Alan Simpson's Easy
Guide to Windows® 95

Alan Simpson's Easy Guide to Windows® 95

Alan Simpson
Elizabeth Olson

SYBEX®

San Francisco · Paris · Düsseldorf · Soest

Acquisitions Manager: Kristine Plachy
Developmental Editor: Richard Mills
Editor: Laura Arendal
Technical Editor: Richard Nollet
Book Designer: Claudia Smelser
Technical Artist: Cuong Le
Desktop Publishing Specialist: Molly Sharp
Production Coordinator: Sarah Lemas
Indexer: Ted Laux
Cover Designer: Joanna Kim Gladden

Screen reproductions produced with Collage Complete.

Collage Complete is a trademark of Inner Media Inc.

SYBEX is a registered trademark of SYBEX Inc.

Library of Congress Card Number: 95-67728
ISBN: 0-7821-1708-2

Manufactured in the United States of America
10 9 8 7 6 5 4 3 2

To Al and Emily Gotkin, my parents, and to Keith Olson, my husband and best friend. Thanks for all your unselfish love and support.

—Elizabeth Olson

Acknowledgments

We'd like to thank the many people at Sybex whose talent, skill, and hard work brought this book from our desktop PCs into your hands. Many thanks to David Kolodney for dreaming up the Easy Guide concept, to Richard Mills for his many valuable suggestions, to Laura Arendal for her meticulous editing and keeping us on schedule, to Technical Reviewer Richard Nollet for keeping our instructions honest, and to Desktop Publishing Specialist Molly Sharp, Production Coordinator Sarah Lemas, and Indexer Ted Laux for all their hard work.

From Alan, many thanks to Susan, Ashley, and Alec for their patience and support.

From Elizabeth, thanks to Keith for waiting patiently while I pound the computer keys into dust and for making life fun.

Contents at a Glance

Table of Contents

CHAPTER 4   Managing Files, Folders, and Objects   43

CHAPTER 5   Using Your Programs   69

CHAPTER **6** **Writing and Painting**   **85**

Introduction

The computer press and other industry pundits like to whine and complain about everything new. So you may have already heard some negative comments about Windows 95. But you won't hear any of those here. We've been using Windows 95 for a long time—since December 1993, to be exact. And that experience has led us to conclude that Windows 95 is the best thing to happen to the PC industry in a long time.

Upgraders can refer to the section *What's New in Windows 95?* below for a more in-depth look at the differences between the old and the new Windows.

You'll see this guy in the margins throughout the book. He has tips, warnings, explanations, examples, helpful anecdotes, and references to further information on a topic.

How This Book Works

For many people, an operating system such as Windows 95 plays two roles: (1) It lets you start whatever program you want to use, and (2) It lets you move, copy, and delete files. These certainly are important topics in this book, but there's more than that.

In this book we're assuming: you don't have any formal training in computer science or programming; you do have a PC or access to one, and you already know the basics of working the mouse and keyboard; and you don't care about the hidden technicalities of Windows 95—you just want to put it to work to make your life easier.

Windows Basics

Chapters 1 through 4 focus on the basic skills and concepts you need to get along with Windows 95. If you've been using

Windows 3.1, some of the new stuff will be confusing at first. But once you get used to doing things in Windows 95, you'll find that the new ways are better and easier.

If you need more information on a particular topic right away, look for me and my map. I'll direct you to areas of the book that discuss a topic in more depth.

Programs and Accessories

Chapters 5 through 8 explore many of the basic skills in much more depth. Here you'll learn alternative ways to do things so you can develop techniques and shortcuts that are relevant to your own work.

Customization and Maintenance

Chapters 9 and 10 will teach you how to customize Windows 95 to your own tastes. You'll learn how to personalize the screen, mouse, and keyboard and how to keep your computer in tip-top shape.

All you need to get started on a journey into cyberspace is a modem.

Connecting to the Outside

In Chapters 11 through 14 we'll show you how to install a modem and plug into the many information services you've probably been hearing about, including the Internet. You'll also learn about the new features designed specifically for laptops and mobile computing.

But enough already about the book. Next we'll discuss the new stuff you'll find in Windows 95.

What's New in Windows 95?

When compared to its predecessor, Windows 95 has a lot to offer:

- Windows 95 is faster and takes full advantage of modern 486 and Pentium PCs.

- Windows 95 is easier to use.

- Windows 95 is easier for beginners to learn.

- Windows 95 has a better built-in Help system.

- Windows 95 wastes less of your time. For example, you can print documents, download files, format floppy disks, and work on your latest project all at the same time!

- Windows 95 is more personal, because you can customize almost *everything* to your liking.

- Windows 95 offers many new features for laptop computers. These features make mobile computing easier and more productive.

Windows 95 sports a whole new *look and feel* that makes it easier (and more fun) to use. Figure 1 shows a typical desktop for Windows 3.1. Compare this with Figure 2, the desktop for Windows 95.

Here's what the most important parts of the Windows 95 desktop are for:

- *My Computer* provides quick access to your computer's disk drives and to the Control Panel and Printers.

This section is mainly for experienced Windows 3.x users who want to know what's new and different in Windows 95. If you're completely new to Windows, feel free to skip it.

Don't let these cosmetic differences throw you! Many of the handy shortcuts that you love in Windows 3.x also work in Windows 95! (Try your favorite shortcut anytime.)

FIGURE 1

*The typical desktop for
Windows 3.1*

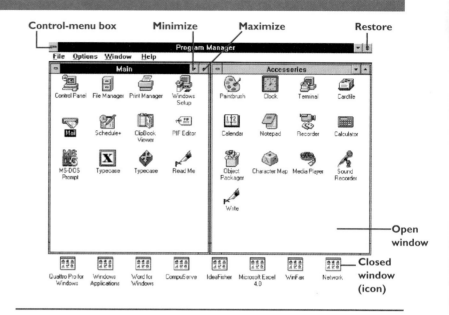

FIGURE 2

*The typical desktop for
Windows 95, with
My Computer and
Network Neighborhood
windows opened. We also
clicked on the Start button
on the taskbar.*

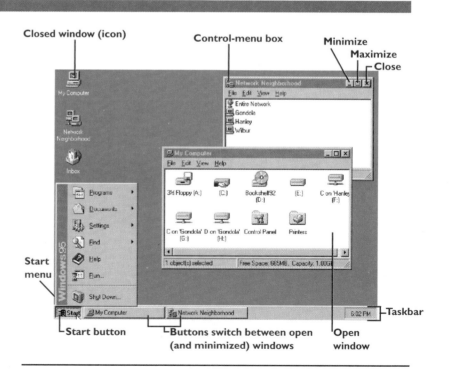

- *Network Neighborhood* lets you explore and work with other computers on your network.

- The *taskbar* lets you switch between opened (or minimized) windows. It also includes the Start button described next.

- The *Start* button on the taskbar lets you start programs, open recently used documents, change settings, find things, get online Help, and shut down your computer.

How Do I...

As an upgrader faced with the Windows 95 desktop for the first time, you'll probably have a million questions. But knowing the answers to just a few key questions will get you up and running with Windows 95 in no time.

How Do I Start Programs?

Easy! Click on the Start button on the taskbar, click on Programs, and then continue clicking on options on the menus until you start the program you want.

You can also start a program by double-clicking. First, double-click on My Computer on the desktop. Next, double-click on disk and folder icons until you see the icon for the program you want to start or the file you want to open. Finally, double-click on that icon. (It's a lot like using File Manager to start a program or open a data file.)

See Chapter 5 for more information on starting programs.

How Do I Manage My Windows?

Closed windows appear as icons on the desktop, and open windows are framed areas. To open a closed window, double-click on its icon (just as in Windows 3.x).

As Figures 1 and 2 show, the Minimize and Maximize buttons look different in Windows 95, but they do the same thing

See Chapters 3 and 4 for more about working with windows and other controls.

when you click on them. To close a window, click on its Close button (X) or double-click on its Control menu icon.

To switch to another opened (or minimized) window, click on the button for that window in the taskbar.

What's This Right-Clicking I've Heard So Much About?

You can right-click on just about anything you can see on the desktop to bring up a menu of options that pertain to the object you right-clicked on. This saves you the trouble of looking for appropriate menu options.

Here are some useful places to right-click:

- To customize the desktop appearance, right-click on an empty area on the desktop and click on Properties.

- To arrange open windows on the desktop, right-click on an empty area of the taskbar and click on Cascade, Tile Horizontally, Tile Vertically, or Minimize All Windows.

- To customize the taskbar or Start menu options, right-click on an empty area on the taskbar and then click on Properties.

What Happened to Program Manager?

Program Manager really isn't needed any longer. To get to your old Program Manager groups, click on Start ➤ Programs. All those groups will appear on the menu that pops up.

What Happened to File Manager?

File Manager is no longer needed either. That's because File Manager and all the browsing and file-management tools it offered are now built right into Windows 95. File Manager's replacement is Windows Explorer (Start ➤ Programs ➤ Windows Explorer).

What Happened to DOS?

DOS itself is gone (yeah!). However, many DOS commands are available for die-hard fans, and DOS programs run fine under Windows 95. To reach the DOS prompt while using Windows, choose Start ➤ Programs ➤ MS-DOS Prompt. When you've finished with the DOS session, type **exit** and press ↵ (just as in the old Windows), or click on the Close (X) button in the MS-DOS Prompt window.

To start your computer without Windows, choose Start ➤ Sh<u>u</u>tdown ➤ *Restart the computer in M<u>S</u>-DOS mode?* ➤ Yes. Or choose Start ➤ Sh<u>u</u>t Down ➤ *Restart the computer?* ➤ <u>Y</u>es. When the *Starting Windows 95* message appears, press F8, choose option 5 or 6, and then press ↵.

How to Find Out More

There's a lot more new stuff in Windows than this brief introduction can offer. To find out more, click on the What's <u>N</u>ew button in the Welcome dialog box that appears when you first start Windows 95, or choose Start ➤ <u>H</u>elp, click on the Contents tab, and double-click on Introducing Windows (see Figure 3). Finally, double-click on any topics you want to know more about.

Now that we've covered what's new in Windows 95, let's get Windows 95 fired up and put that pup to work!

If you specifically want to get to the Welcome dialog box, click on the Start button, choose <u>R</u>un, type **welcome**, and choose OK.

FIGURE 3

Windows Help

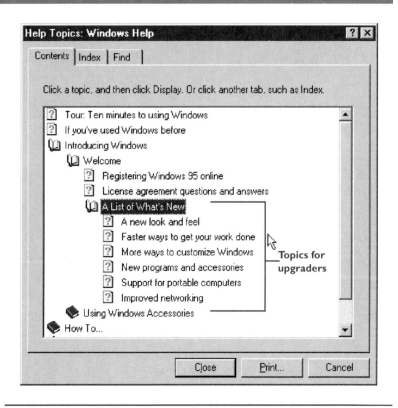

Introducing Windows 95

Featuring

- What is Windows 95?
- Windows 95 for beginners
- Windows 95 for experienced users
- What Windows 95 can do for you
- Where to go from here

In the olden days of personal computing, you had to be part computer expert and part magician to make the PC do *anything* at all (let alone do anything useful). But thanks to Windows 95, the PC is becoming a simple, intuitive tool that everyone can use.

What Is Windows 95?

Windows 95 is the latest and greatest *operating system* for the IBM PC (and PC clone) family of computers. An operating system is the program that determines how you, the user, *operate* the computer.

Actually, Windows 95 comes with some simple, though useful, word-processing, graphics, and other programs. We'll introduce those at the end of this chapter.

The operating system is different from other types of computer programs in a couple of big ways. For one, an operating system is *required.* Your computer won't work at all if it doesn't have an operating system on it.

Another thing that makes the operating system unique is that it's not designed to help you do any specific type of work. Rather, the operating system gives you access to other programs (see Table 1.1) and also provides general tools for fine-tuning and managing your PC. Some of the possibilities are summarized later in this chapter.

TABLE 1.1

Categories and Brand Names of Some Popular PC Programs

Popular Type (Category) of Program	What It Helps You Do	Brand Names
Word Processing	Type letters, write memos, and publish newsletters and books	WordPerfect, Word, Ami Pro
Spreadsheet	Juggle numbers for budgets, projections, and financial models	1-2-3, Excel, Quattro Pro
Database	Store and retrieve information, such as customer lists, invoices, or a family tree	dBASE, Paradox, Access, Approach
Presentation	Create public presentations, including slides, overheads, and notes	PowerPoint, WordPerfect Presentations

Popular Type (Category) of Program	What It Helps You Do	Brand Names	**TABLE 1.1**
			Categories and Brand Names of Some Popular PC Programs (continued)
Education/ Multimedia/ Games	Educate the kids, look up facts and figures, or just kill time	Reader Rabbit, Just Grandma and Me, Microsoft Bookshelf, DOOM	
Operating Systems	Install and use all of the above on your PC	Windows 95, DOS, Windows 3.1, OS/2 Warp, Unix	

Windows 95 for Beginners

If you've never used a computer or Windows before, the very thought of using a PC might seem pretty scary. Much of that fear comes from all the mysterious jargon that computer people use. Terms like *megabytes*, *DOS*, *memory*, and so forth might mean absolutely nothing to you. Don't worry about that. You can start using your PC productively today, even if you don't know a *monitor* from a tunafish sandwich.

Half the people who banter around a lot of tech talk really don't know what they're talking about. They're just out to impress you. Another good reason not to let techno-jargon intimidate you!

Don't Let the Jargon Scare Ya

We know how intimidating unfamiliar jargon can be. Once Alan went to the doctor because he had a stiff neck. After examining his neck, the doctor wrote *Torticollis* as the diagnosis. (Yikes! Sounds serious!) Fearing the worst, Alan sheepishly asked what that meant. The doctor replied, "It means you have a stiff neck." (Gee, thanks, Doc. I knew that before I came here.) The point is that, more often than not, a buzzword that sounds serious and difficult to grasp turns out to be no big deal when you find out what it really means.

We'll tell you what all the buzzwords mean if, and when, it becomes necessary. To get you started, Figure 1.1 shows you the names of the various doodads that make up a typical desktop PC (by the way, PC is short for *personal computer*).

FIGURE 1.1

The parts of a PC

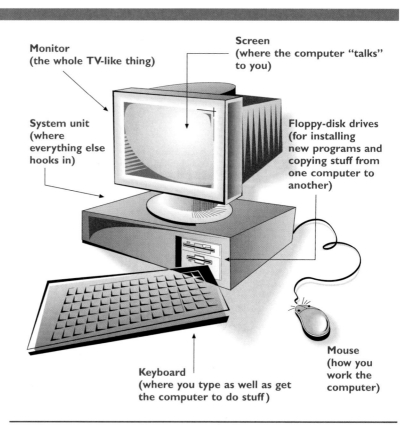

Monitor (the whole TV-like thing)

Screen (where the computer "talks" to you)

System unit (where everything else hooks in)

Floppy-disk drives (for installing new programs and copying stuff from one computer to another)

Keyboard (where you type as well as get the computer to do stuff)

Mouse (how you work the computer)

Here are the names of the various gadgets that make up a "typical" desktop PC. Don't worry if your PC doesn't look exactly like this one.

It's certainly possible to *delete* information from a PC, but you have to jump through a few hoops to do it. It's not the kind of thing that you're likely to do by accident.

If you're afraid of computers because you worry that you'll do something wrong, like break the machine or wipe out someone's treasured information, stop worrying. There's almost nothing you can do to break a PC (short of throwing it out a window).

If you are new to PCs, you can just skip the next section, which is written for experienced users who want to know how Windows 95 compares to Windows 3.1. Ignore all that if you're new to PCs.

Windows 95 for Experienced Users

If you're an experienced Windows 3.1 user, your big concerns are probably: (1) will my existing Windows (and DOS) programs still work, and (2) do I really want to learn yet another new way of doing things?

The answer to the first question is a simple: "Yes." You can use all your existing DOS and Windows applications in Windows 95.

As far as the second question goes, we'd again say: "Yes." Even though it *is* a pain to learn a new way of doing things, it's worth it if there's some benefit. There are plenty of benefits to switching to Windows 95—the most immediate one being the amount of effort it takes to get from point A to point B for most tasks. Let's look at an example.

Let's say that in Windows 3.1 you're at the Program Manager and want to open a Word document that you started yesterday. To do so you might go through this scenario:

● Double-click on Word's group icon.

● Double-click on Word's application icon and wait.

● Choose File ➤ Open, double-click on the name of the file you want to open, then wait.

Not the most strenuous activity in the world. But it does involve a half-dozen mouse clicks and some waiting in between.

Trust us. Once you get used to the new Windows 95 way of doing things, you'll probably never want to see the old Program Manager again.

Now here's how you might do that same task in Windows 95:

- Click on the Start button and point to Documents.
- Click on the name of the document you want to open.

That's only two clicks, without any waiting in between.

What Windows 95 Can Do for You

It's not necessary to read this entire book before you start using Windows 95. In fact, it's not necessary to read this entire book at all. After you learn the basic skills you need to get around in Windows (Chapter 2), you can look up and learn about topics at your own pace.

If you're not even sure what kinds of topics you might want to explore, here's a list of just some of the things you can do with Windows 95.

- Do simple *word processing* with WordPad. For example, you can write quick notes, letters, memos, and so forth.
- Create logos and pictures using Paint.
- Do day-to-day math with the on-screen Calculator.
- Schedule appointments and get organized with WinPad and Cardfile.
- Play games (Windows 95 comes with several!).
- Back up data onto floppy disks or tape.
- Speed up your hard disk and squeeze more data into less space.
- Find and fix errors on your computer's hard disk.
- Run all the optional programs installed on your computer and install new programs.

If you have a modem attached to your computer, you can also

- Auto-dial your phone.

- Explore cyberspace—with services like America Online, CompuServe, Prodigy, and the Internet.

- Send and receive electronic mail and faxes.

If you have two or more computers, you might want to learn how to

- Keep your desktop and laptop computers in sync using Briefcase.

- Network your computers so you can share printers and files.

As with any book, you can look up information on any topic, at your convienence, in the Table of Contents in the front or the Index at the back of this book.

A *modem* is a gadget that hooks your computer to a telephone jack. Some computers come with modems built in.

Where to Go from Here

Now that you have some idea about the power that Windows 95 will give you, it's time to take Windows for a hands-on test drive. Turn to Chapter 2. Once you've taken the Windows 95 spin, you can jump to just about any place in this book that interests you.

If you're new to PCs, go straight to Chapter 2. If you're an experienced Windows 3.1 user, you can skim through *What's New in Windows 95* in the Introduction to this book to see what's new. Then come back and read Chapter 2 to get a feel for the new Windows 95 interface.

CHAPTER 2

Getting Your Fingers Wet

Featuring

- Starting Windows 95
- About the Windows desktop
- How to use the mouse
- How to use the keyboard
- How to take the Windows Tour
- When it's safe to turn off your computer

The best way to learn to use Windows 95, and your PC in general, is to just do it. This chapter will give you a hands-on guided tour of everything from starting your PC, to using it, to shutting down your system. So pull up a chair, make yourself comfy, and try to spend a half an hour or so without any interruptions while learning to use your PC.

How to Start Windows 95

See Figure 1.1 in Chapter 1 if you're not sure what the monitor, system unit, and so forth are.

Starting Windows 95 is just a matter of turning on your computer. For you neophytes, here's how to do that:

1. Remove any disks from your computer's floppy disk drives.

2. Turn on the monitor, printer, and any other devices that are hooked to the system unit. Turn on the system unit last.

3. Wait a minute or so. You may see a little activity on the screen and system unit. Don't worry, that's normal.

4. If your computer is connected to a local network, you'll see a *dialog box* like the one shown here. If your network adminstrator has told you how to fill out the dialog box, do so. Otherwise, just press Escape.

When we say *press Escape,* that means *press the key labeled Esc or Cancel.* That key is usually near the upper-left corner of the keyboard.

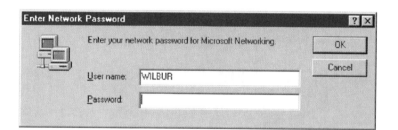

5. Eventually, you'll see the Windows *desktop* looking something like the example shown in Figure 2.1.

If the Welcome dialog box appears on your screen, press Escape or click on the Close button with your mouse to close it for now. Don't worry if the Welcome dialog box isn't there. Someone may have just turned it off.

FIGURE 2.1

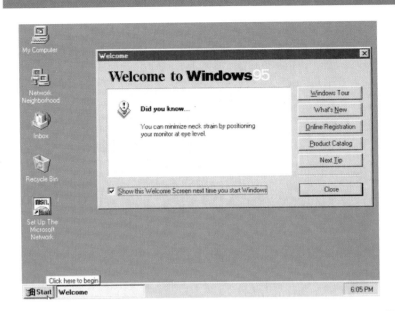

The desktop with the Welcome dialog box visible

If your screen doesn't look *anything* like Figure 2.1, your PC might have a different operating system—such as DOS, Windows 3, or OS/2 Warp—installed. If so, move straight to the Appendix.

About the Windows Desktop

The Windows 95 desktop will be your "home base" whenever you use your computer. The desktop gets its name from the fact that it's sort of like your "real" (wooden) desktop. But there are a couple of important differences:

- On your real desktop, you usually shuffle papers around. On the Windows desktop, you shuffle *windows* and *icons* around.

- On your real desktop, you use your bare hands to shuffle things around. On the Windows desktop, you use the mouse to shuffle things around.

Taskbar and Start Button

The strip along the bottom of the desktop is called the *taskbar*. We'll talk about the many conveniences that the taskbar offers a little later in this chapter. But for now, just notice that at the left side of the taskbar there's a button labeled *Start*.

How to Use the Mouse

Those of you who have never used a mouse before might already be feeling queasy about all this clicking and so forth. So before we go any further, let's discuss how you use a mouse. First, just place your hand comfortably over the mouse with your index finger resting gently on (not pushing on) the leftmost (*primary*) mouse button, as shown in Figure 2.2.

If you're left-handed, you can make the rightmost button (the one under your index finger) the primary button and the leftmost button the secondary button. Choose Start ➤ Settings ➤ Control Panel. Double-click on the Mouse icon, choose Left-Handed, then OK.

If you have a *mouse pad*, put the mouse (and your hand) on the pad. A mouse pad is just a sheet of neoprene rubber that offers better traction than a wooden desktop. The things you do with the mouse are summarized below.

Point   Move the mouse pointer so it's touching some object.

Click   Point to an object then press and release the leftmost mouse button.

Double-click   Point to an object and click the leftmost mouse button twice in rapid succession. This technique is usually used to *open* an object.

Right-click   Point to an object and click the rightmost button.

Drag   Point to an object and hold down the mouse button while moving the mouse.

You'll have a chance to practice those things when you take the hands-on tutorial a little later in this chapter.

FIGURE 2.2

How to hold the mouse

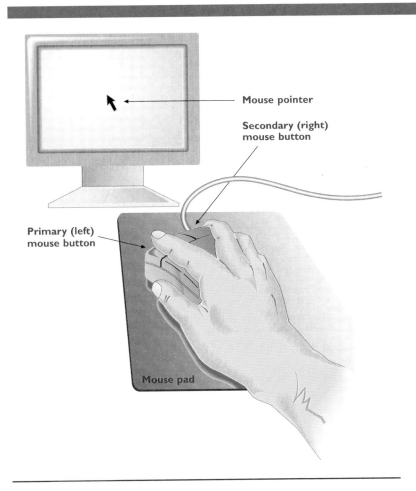

Mouse pointer

Secondary (right)
mouse button

Primary (left)
mouse button

Mouse pad

How to Use the Keyboard

Most of the keyboard is laid out like a normal typewriter's keyboard. Those typewriter keys let you type whenever there's a reason to type on the screen. As you'll see, the screen usually takes regular typewriting when there's whitespace to type on.

In addition to the regular typewriter keys, the keyboard contains the special keys described on the next page.

If pressing Escape doesn't back you out of unfamiliar territory, closing the unfamiliar window will usually do the trick. As you'll learn later, you can close any window by clicking on the X button in the upper-right corner of the window you want to close.

Escape   The Escape key is usually labeled Esc or Cancel and is generally in the upper-left corner of the keyboard. It's aptly named because pressing it often lets you *escape* from unfamiliar territory. A good general rule to keep in mind is, "If in doubt, Escape key out!"

Function Keys   The function keys labeled F1 through F12 do a variety of jobs that you'll learn about as you go through this book. For now it's sufficient to know that when you see an instruction like *press F5*, it means *press the function key labeled F5*. Don't type the letter F and then the number 5.

Enter, or Return, Key   Some people call this key the Enter key because it *enters* whatever you typed on the screen. Other people call it the Return key because it's in the same place as the Carriage Return key on a typewriter. It's often marked with a ↵ symbol because on a typewriter it jumps down a line and moves back to the left.

Tab   The Tab key plays the dual role of indenting text (when you're typing) and moving from one prompt to another when you're faced with several prompts. You'll see examples as we go along. For now, just try to locate it on your keyboard. It might be marked with two opposing arrows rather than the word Tab. But usually it's just to the left of the letter Q.

Don't even try to hit both keys at the same time.

Key+Key   You'll often come across an instruction to press a *combination keystroke*, represented as *key+key*. Some examples include Shift+Tab or Ctrl+A or Alt+F1. The Shift, Alt, and Ctrl keys are usually grouped together near the lower-left and lower-right corners of the typing keys, within easy reach of your pinkie. To press a combination keystroke, you hold down the first key, tap the second key, then release the first key. For example, to press Alt+S you'd hold down the Alt key, tap the letter S, then release the Alt key.

Why Mouse and Keyboard?

There's a mouse method and a keyboard method for doing just about everything. Some people find this over-lap confusing, but it's really just a way of accommodating different types of people. If you're a good typist and most of your work involves writing and typing, you'll probably want to use the keyboard most of the time. Hence, there's a keyboard method for doing just about everything.

On the other hand, if your work involves drawing and designing, or you just can't type worth beans, you'll probably prefer to use the mouse. Neither method is particularly "better than" the other. It's just a matter of personal preference.

Now that you know how to work the mouse and keyboard, let's try putting those newfound skills to use.

Taking the Hands-On Tour

You're now ready to take the official hands-on tour. Follow these steps:

- If you see the Welcome screen on your desktop, just click on the <u>W</u>indows Tour button.

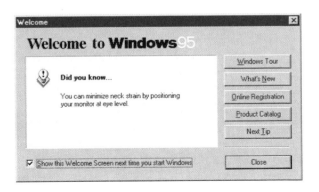

If you installed Windows 95 from a CD-ROM, you may be prompted to insert the CD-ROM before you can run the tour. To continue, insert the Windows 95 CD-ROM and then click on OK. Or, if the CD-ROM is not available at the moment, click on Cancel or press Escape to skip the tour for now.

If you installed Windows 95 from a CD-ROM, you may be prompted to insert it before you can run the tour. If you installed from floppies and Windows can't find the tour, install it now from Supplemental Disk 1 (see the Appendix).

● If you *don't* see the Welcome screen, click on the Start button and then click on Run. Type the word **welcome**, then click on OK. Now you can click on the Windows Tour button in the Welcome screen.

You should be at the screen shown in Figure 2.3. Using the basic mouse and keyboard skills you've learned up to now, follow the instructions that appear on the screen to take the guided tour. Ignore the rest of this chapter until you've completed the lessons in the tour. Then read the section that follows.

FIGURE 2.3

The hands-on guided tour starts right here.

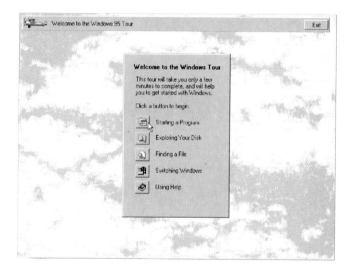

If you're new to PCs, we strongly recommend that you take each lesson several times until you can complete the lesson without using the *Show me* button. If you're an experienced Windows 3.1 user, we still recommend that you run through the tutorial. After spending just a few minutes with the tour, you'll get a feel for Windows 95.

When It's Safe to Turn Off Your Computer

Before you turn off your computer, it's *essential* to shut down Windows 95. Doing so protects any unsaved information from loss.

Shutting down is easy. Just follow these steps:

1 Click on the Start button and choose Sh<u>u</u>t Down. You'll see the *Shut down Windows* dialog box (Figure 2.4).

FIGURE 2.4

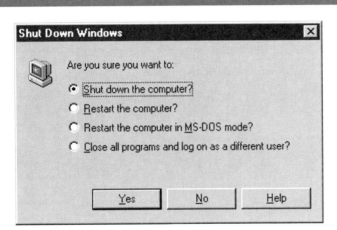

The Shut down Windows dialog box lets you exit Windows gracefully and save any unsaved work before you turn off the computer.

2 Choose one of these shutdown options:

- If you plan to turn off the computer, click on *Shut down the computer?* (This option is selected automatically.)

- If you want Windows to start the computer again without turning off the power first, click on *Restart the computer?*

- If you want Windows to restart the computer and leave you at the DOS prompt instead of the Windows desktop, click on *Restart the computer in MS-DOS mode?* After working at the DOS prompt, you can return to Windows by typing win and pressing ↵.

Sometimes this option is handy if Windows is behaving strangely and you need to restart with a clean slate.

● If you're on a network and want to sign on with a different user name, click on *Close all programs and log on as a different user?*

3 Click on the Yes button and wait patiently.

4 If you've left any unsaved work behind, you'll be asked if you want to save it. To save your work, choose Yes, then specify a file name in the Save As dialog box (see Chapter 5) and choose Save. To shut down without saving, choose No.

5 If you chose *Shut down the computer?* in step 2, turn off the power when Windows says it's safe to do so. If you chose one of the other options, respond to any sign-on prompts that appear (as explained at the start of this chapter).

CHAPTER 3

Windows Basics

Featuring

- Using the taskbar
- Using menus
- Starting and stopping programs
- Juggling your windows
- Using scroll bars
- Using dialog boxes
- Using toolbars

Chapter 2 gave you a hands-on tour of starting, getting around in, and shutting down Windows 95. From here on, we'll assume you know how to do all that stuff, including things like clicking, double-clicking, right-clicking, pressing *key+key* combination keystrokes, and so forth. If all that sounds like Greek to you, then you probably skipped Chapter 2 (or maybe your dog ate it for breakfast). If that's the case, we suggest you go back there now so you don't get totally lost halfway through this chapter.

You don't need to be at the keyboard while reading the rest of these chapters. You can practice what you learn here when you get back to the PC.

Using the Taskbar

The taskbar, as we've mentioned, is sort of like a desk drawer where you can keep things handy without actually having them clutter the screen. The all-important Start button is also on the taskbar. Figure 3.1 shows the taskbar with some icons for open windows already in it.

FIGURE 3.1

The taskbar with important features illustrated

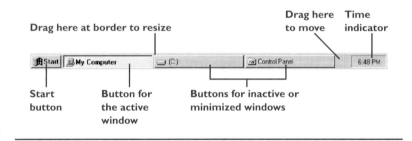

Drag here at border to resize

Drag here to move   Time indicator

Start button

Button for the active window

Buttons for inactive or minimized windows

From time to time, other indicators will appear at the edge of the taskbar next to the time indicator. For more information about an indicator, point to that indicator with your mouse (for instance, try pointing to the current time indicator). To open or adjust the indicator, double-click on it. To see all options for an indicator, right-click on the indicator.

Using the Start Button

As the name implies, the Start button is the perfect place to start just about anything you want to do on your PC. You can click on the Start button or press Ctrl+Esc to open the Start button's menu.

Table 3.1 briefly explains what each option on the Start menu can do for you. *Using Menus*, later in the chapter, explains how to use any menu, including the Windows 95 Start menu.

TABLE 3.1

Windows 95 Start menu options explained

Menu Name	What It Does
Programs	Lets you start a program
Documents	Lets you open recently saved documents
Settings	Lets you personalize Windows in a variety of ways (see Chapter 9)
Find	Lets you search for Files or Folders, or a Computer on your network (see Chapters 5 and 12)
Help	Opens the Help that comes with Windows (see Chapter 2)
Run	Offers a way to run a program that has no icon on the Start menus

Moving and Resizing the Taskbar

Initially the taskbar appears at the bottom edge of the desktop, but you can place it at any edge you like. To do so, move the mouse pointer to an empty part of the taskbar, then drag the outline to the edge you want.

To resize the taskbar narrower or wider, move the mouse pointer to the long edge of the taskbar that's closest to the center of the desktop. When the mouse pointer changes to a two-headed arrow, drag the taskbar up or down (if the taskbar is at the bottom or top edge of the desktop) or to the left or right (if the taskbar is at the right or left edge).

You'll probably be happiest with the taskbar at the top or bottom edge of the desktop, where it takes up the least space.

Other Taskbar and Start-Button Properties

In addition to moving and sizing the taskbar, you can change some of the characteristics (properties) of how it behaves:

1 Right-click on the taskbar and choose Properties from the pop-up menu.

2 If the Taskbar Options tab isn't already selected, click on it.

3 Set the following properties as you wish. When you select an item, the sample picture in the dialog box will give you a preview of what to expect when you return to the desktop:

Always on top: When selected, the taskbar is always fully visible at the bottom of the screen. If cleared (deselected), other windows can cover the taskbar. Pressing Ctrl+Esc will bring the taskbar out of hiding and open the Start menu as well.

Auto Hide: If you select both *Always on top* and *Auto hide*, the taskbar is reduced to a barely visible thin line at the bottom of the screen when you're not using it. To display the taskbar, you just need to move the mouse pointer to the very bottom of the screen (no need to press Ctrl+Esc).

Show small icons in Start menu: Reduces the size of the Start menu by eliminating the Windows 95 banner and showing smaller icons.

Show Clock: If you select Show Clock, the current system time will appear at the edge of the taskbar (see Figure 3.1). If you deselect this option, the current system time won't appear on the taskbar.

4 Choose OK to return to the desktop.

If the taskbar covers information you're accustomed to seeing, or you find yourself selecting taskbar options by accident, try using it with the Always on top and Auto hide features turned on.

Switching between Programs and Windows

After you've opened several windows on the desktop, you can switch quickly to the window you want by clicking on its button in the taskbar. The currently selected window (or *active window*) will have a colored title bar and will appear on top of other windows. Its button will appear pushed in on the taskbar. You can also bring any window to the forefront simply by clicking on any visible portion of that window.

For example, in Figure 3.2 the Calculator program is in the active window, and its taskbar button is pushed in.

FIGURE 3.2

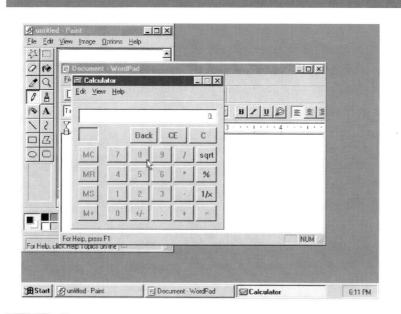

Click on a button in the taskbar to switch quickly to another open window.

To switch to the Paint window in this example, you'd just press the *untitled - Paint* button in the taskbar.

If you prefer to use the keyboard to switch between windows, you can:

- Press Alt+Esc. Each time you press Alt+Esc, the next available open window will appear in front and that window's button will be pushed in on the taskbar.

- Press Alt+Tab to display a dialog box of icons for all open windows. If you keep the Alt key held down and press the Tab key, the selection box will move from one

Actually, each time you press Alt+Esc, the high-light moves to the next button in the taskbar. If there is no open window for the current button, then all you'll see is the taskbar button highlighted. Pressing ↵, however, will then open that window.

icon to the next. Releasing the Alt key brings the currently selected window to the forefront.

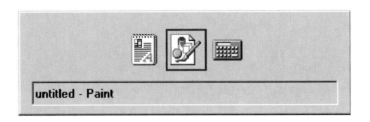

More Clever Shortcuts with the Taskbar

The taskbar is as versatile as a circus seal. Here are some more things you can do with it:

- Right-click on an empty area of the taskbar, then choose an option from the property sheet that pops up. These options let you arrange the open windows quickly without having to drag them around on the screen. The last option, Properties, lets you customize the taskbar.

- Right-click on a button in the taskbar and choose property-sheet options for restoring, moving, sizing, minimizing, maximizing, or closing the window. Right-clicking on the Start button displays a property sheet with options for opening the Start menu's Programs folder, exploring your computer and network, and finding files or folders quickly.

- Double-click on the time indicator to change your computer's date, time, and time-zone settings.

Using Menus

Menus make it easy for you to get work done in Windows because you don't have to type or memorize anything. Just cruise through the menus until you find what you want, click on an option, and away you go. Much easier than typing the arcane commands you may have worked with in other operating systems such as DOS!

Chapter 2 gave you some practice using menus by clicking on options with your mouse. In this section you'll learn general ways to work with menus using either the mouse or keyboard.

Opening a Menu

Windows 95 provides you with three types of menus:

Start menu on the taskbar: Appears when you click on the Start button on the taskbar or press Ctrl+Esc. You saw several examples of this menu in Chapter 1.

Menu on a menu bar: Appears when you choose an option from a window's menu bar (see Figure 3.3). This kind of menu is called a *pulldown menu* because when you open it, it "pulls down" like a window shade. To open a pulldown menu, click on the menu you want in the appropriate menu bar (for example, click on File in the menu bar in Figure 3.3). If you prefer to use your keyboard, first make sure the window is active. Then...

- Press Alt and type the underlined letter of the menu you want to open (for example, Alt+F opens the File menu).

- Or press Alt, then press the ← or → keys on your keyboard to highlight the menu you want, and then press ↵.

Property-sheet menus: Pertain to a specific item. To open a property-sheet menu (or more simply, a property sheet), right-click on the item you're interested in.

FIGURE 3.3

The different ways to get to menus

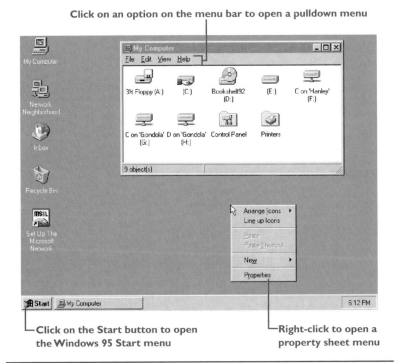

Click on an option on the menu bar to open a pulldown menu

Click on the Start button to open the Windows 95 Start menu

Right-click to open a property sheet menu

Whether you use the mouse or keyboard is purely a personal preference. If your hand is on the mouse at the moment, just use the mouse. If you happen to be typing when you want to open a menu, use the keyboard instead. That way, you won't have to take your fingers off the keyboard.

Choosing Menu Options

Once you've opened a menu, there are a bunch of ways you can choose options on the menu. If you like using the mouse, here's what to do:

- If the option is marked with a ➤, point to or click on the option. Another menu will open.

- If the option is not marked with a ➤, click on the option. This will carry out the command you selected.

If the keyboard is more your style…

- If the option is marked with a ➤, highlight it by pressing the ↑ or ↓ keys, then press the → key on your keyboard, or you can type the *hotkey*—the underlined letter—of the option. Another menu will open.

● If the option is not marked with a ➤, type the underlined letter of the option or highlight the option and press the ↵ key. This will carry out the command.

What's on the Menu?

Some menu options might have markings other than the ➤ symbol. Some markings you might come across include ellipses (...), which lead to a dialog box, or *key* or *key+key*, which indicates a shortcut key—or keys—you can press to get to the option without going through the menus. A check mark (✔) or dot (•) indicates that an option is currently activated (turned on). Selecting that option will deactivate (turn off) the option. A menu option that's dimmed isn't available for selection simply because it's not appropriate for what you're trying to do at the moment.

Backing Out of Menus

You'll probably open a menu by accident, or open the wrong menu, from time to time. Not to worry—you can use any of these techniques to back out of a menu without making a selection:

● Click on an empty area outside the menu.

● Press Escape (Esc) to close just the current menu.

● Press Alt to close a whole series of menus.

What Does *That* Option Do?

Some programs show their menu-option descriptions at the top, rather than the bottom, of the application's window. To explore, just click on any option in the program's menu bar and move the mouse pointer through the menu options. Look for changing descriptions near the top, or bottom, of that program's window.

When you're using the pulldown menus in a program and you're not sure what a particular option does, just highlight the option you're curious about and take a peek at the status bar near the bottom of that program's window. You'll see a brief description of the currently highlighted option. (In many programs, pressing F1 will display even more information.)

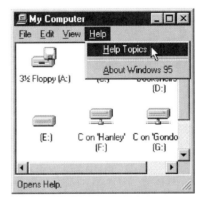

Starting and Stopping Programs

Table 1.1 in Chapter 1 summarizes some types and brand names of a few popular PC programs.

Programs are what let you do work, or have fun, with your PC. And Windows is your home base from which you start all programs.

Starting a Program

There are several techniques you can use to launch a program from the Windows 95 desktop:

● If you see an icon labeled *Shortcut to <the name of the program you want to start>*, you can just double-click on that icon.

● If the program has an icon on the Start menu, choose Start and then the name of the program.

● If the program isn't on the Start menu, choose Start ➤ Programs, then explore the various groups on the Programs menu until you find the program you want.

● If you recently used a program to create and save a document, try choosing Start ➤ Documents. If you see the name of the document you saved in the Documents menu, click on that name. The appropriate program will start and automatically load the document you requested.

● If there is no icon for the program you want to start, choose Start ➤ Run, then type the location and name of the program you want to start. For example, to install a new program, you typically put its floppy disk in drive A, choose Start ➤ Run, and then type in **a:\setup** or **a:\install**. Choose OK to run the program's installation program.

Not all programs can update the Documents list in Windows 95  when you save your work. If you don't find the document you've recently saved in the Documents menu, you can open the program you used to create that document, then use the File menu within that program to reopen your document.

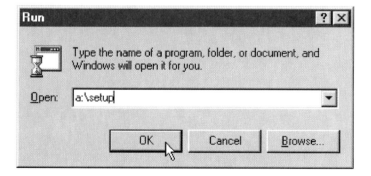

When you install a new Windows program on your PC, the installation procedure will usually create an icon for starting that program. However, when you install a new DOS program, it probably won't create an icon; hence you may need to use Start ➤ Run to start that program.

● You can search for a program's icon by name or use My Computer to go exploring. Either way, once you get to the program's icon, simply double-click on that icon or right-click on it and choose <u>O</u>pen. For a refresher on searching for programs, see Chapter 2.

For example, to start the Mshearts program on this screen, you'd just double-click on its icon.

Stopping a Program

Once you've started a program, you can use it for as long as you wish. When you've finished and want to save any work you've done, use any of these techniques to close the program's window:

Remember: while you're in a program, pressing the Fl key will usually open up Help for that program.

● Click on the Close button (X) in the upper-right corner of the program's window.

● Make sure the program window is active and then press Alt+F4.

● Choose <u>F</u>ile ➤ E<u>x</u>it from the program's menu bar.

● Right-click on the button for the program in the taskbar and choose <u>C</u>lose.

- Double-click on the Control-menu icon at the upper-left corner of the window.

If you haven't saved your most recent changes, you'll be asked if you want to save them. To exit and save the changes, click on the <u>Y</u>es button or type y, enter a file name (see Chapter 4), and click on OK. To exit without saving, click on <u>N</u>o or type n. To return to the program without saving, click on Cancel or press the Esc key.

Shutting Down a Misbehaving Program

Every once in a while a program will *hang* (stop working) for no obvious reason. The computer will seem to freeze, and you won't be able to do anything. If this happens, your only alternative may be to shut down the offending program. But *before* you do this, check the following:

- Is the program doing something that naturally takes a long time? Even on computers, some activities take a long time. If the disk-activity light on the system unit is flashing or you hear some clicking and clacking, the program is probably just busy. Give it a little time before doing anything drastic.

- Is the program asking you to supply some information? Look carefully at the screen. If a dialog box is prompting you for information, complete the dialog box and click on OK or press ↵. If you're not sure what to type, try clicking on the Cancel or Close button (X), or press the Esc key. The program will probably revive.

If you're certain the program is dead as a doornail, press Ctrl+Alt+Del. You'll see a Close Program dialog box like the one in Figure 3.4.

When you see a message or dialog box asking if you want to save your work, don't just choose <u>N</u>o to get rid of the message. If you want to be able to return to what you were just working on, at *any* time in the future, choose <u>Y</u>es and follow all the instructions that appear on the screen.

FIGURE 3.4

*The Close Program
dialog box*

Use this *only* if a
program is hope-
lessly stuck.
Follow the
instructions
carefully to
avoid losing
work.

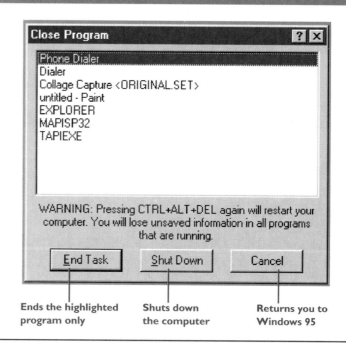

Close Program   ? X

Phone Dialer
Dialer
Collage Capture <ORIGINAL.SET>
untitled - Paint
EXPLORER
MAPISP32
TAPIEXE

WARNING: Pressing CTRL+ALT+DEL again will restart your
computer. You will lose unsaved information in all programs
that are running.

[End Task]   [Shut Down]   [Cancel]

Ends the highlighted   **Shuts down**   **Returns you to**
program only   **the computer**   **Windows 95**

Here's what to do next:

- To change your mind and return to Windows without shutting down any programs, click on Cancel or press Esc.

- To shut down a specific program, click on it in the list, then click on End Task and follow any additional instructions that appear.

- To shut down Windows, click on Shut Down. Windows will shut down all open programs gracefully (prompting you to save any unsaved work if necessary). You can then turn off the computer or restart it by pressing Ctrl+Alt+Del.

- To restart your computer from scratch without saving any work in a graceful manner, press Ctrl+Alt+Del again. *Avoid this last-ditch option if you can.*

Juggling Your Windows

If you took the hands-on guided tour as suggested in
Chapter 2, you've already had some exposure to the tools
for moving and sizing windows. To refresh your memory,
Figure 3.5 shows two windows opened on the desktop and
points out each part of the windows' anatomies.

FIGURE 3.5

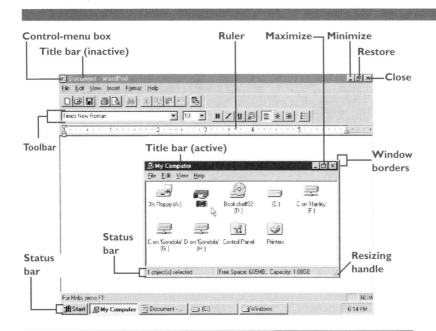

*Two opened windows with
all their body parts labeled*

Moving and Sizing from the Keyboard

If you don't want to take your hands off the keyboard
to move or size a window, you can press Alt+Spacebar
(hold down the Alt key and tap the Spacebar) to open
the program's Control menu. Then choose a sizing
option from that menu. If you choose <u>M</u>ove or <u>S</u>ize, you
can then use the ↑, ↓, →, and ← keys to move or size
the window. Press ↵ when you're done.

- To *move* a window out of the way if it's covering something you want to see, drag the window's title bar to a new position on the desktop (of course, the rest of the window will follow along).

- To *size* a window narrower, wider, taller, or shorter, move the mouse pointer to the resizing handle or to any corner or border. When the pointer changes to a two-headed arrow, drag until the window outline is the size you want, then release the mouse button.

- To *minimize* the window and hide it temporarily, click on its Minimize button. (You can open the window again by clicking on its button in the taskbar.)

- To *maximize* the window so that it fills the entire desktop, click on its Maximize button (the button will change to a Restore button) or double-click on the window's title bar.

- To *restore* the window to its previous size, click on its Restore button (the button will change to a Maximize button) or double-click on the window's title bar.

- To *close* the window, click on its Close button or make sure the window is active (highlighted) and then press Alt+F4. If a program was running in the window, that program will quit (though you may be prompted to save your work). The window will disappear from the desktop, and its button will disappear from the taskbar.

To *organize all the open windows* on your desktop, right-click on an empty area of the taskbar and click on Cascade, Tile Horizontally, Tile Vertically, or Minimize All Windows. If you need to undo your latest *organize all* command, right-click on an empty area of the taskbar and click on the Undo option.

Scroll bars appear only when they're needed. If no scroll bar appears, it's most likely because there's nothing out of view at the moment!

Using Scroll Bars

Scroll bars, like those shown in Figure 3.6, will appear if a window isn't large enough to display everything inside or when a list is too long or too wide to fit within a dialog box. You can use the scroll bars to view additional (or different) information and to get a quick idea of how much information is currently visible.

FIGURE 3.6

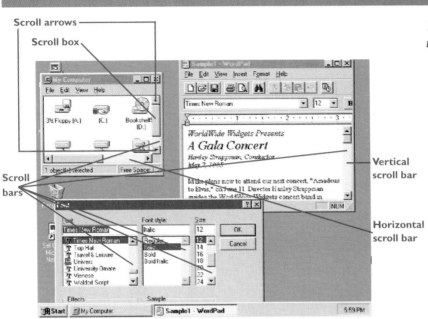

Examples of scroll bars in windows and a dialog box

Just looking at the scroll bars can tell you a lot about how much information is currently visible. The *position of the box* within the scroll bar indicates your current position within the window or list. The *size of the box* tells you how much of the total document or list is visible.

Using scroll bars is easy:

- To scroll through a line at a time, click on the small arrow buttons at either end of the scroll bar. (If the box is touching an arrow button, click on the arrow button *opposite* the box.) Keyboard addicts can press the ↑ and ↓ or ← and → keys instead.

- To scroll a chunk at a time, click on an empty part of the scroll bar. Pressing the Page Up (PgUp) or Page Down (PgDn) keys works as well.

- To scroll smoothly through the window or list, drag the scroll box in the direction you want to scroll.

You can press Ctrl+Home to jump to the top of the scroll bar or press Ctrl+End to jump to the bottom.

Using Dialog Boxes

Dialog boxes (also called *dialogs*) appear whenever you need to make choices or supply more information to a program. Like a window, a dialog box can be dragged by its title bar if you need to move it to see something behind it. But unlike a window, a dialog box is insistent: you can't get out of a dialog box until you choose OK or another button (to proceed) or Cancel (to back out).

Each dialog box contains objects called *controls* (or *options*) that let you do things in the dialog box. The appearance of each control indicates what you can do with that control. Figure 3.7 shows a typical dialog box and its controls. Notice that each control is labeled to let you know what it's for, and most labels include an underlined letter (the *hotkey*). If a control appears dimmed, it's unavailable and you can't use it (that's because it wouldn't make sense at the moment).

If the dialog box has a ? (help) button near the upper-right corner, you can click on that button and then click on any control in the dialog box to learn more about that control.

Selecting Controls

Your mouse offers the easiest and most intuitive way to work with controls. Thus, to select a control you just click on it. For some controls, such as sliders, you drag the control instead.

Here are a few keyboard methods for using controls:

If you use the keyboard to work a dialog box, be aware that the key you press will affect only the currently selected control. (The selected control will be highlighted or framed.) You can press Tab to move forward through controls and Shift+Tab to move backward through them.

- To move to a control, press Tab (to move forward) or Shift+Tab (to move backward) until you highlight the control you want. If this takes you to a group of options, you can then press arrow keys to move the highlight within the group. Pressing the Spacebar will turn a check box on or off.

- To move to a control, or select a command button, or select or deselect a check box, hold down the Alt key while typing the underlined letter (Alt+*letter*). If the insertion point isn't in a text box, you won't need to hold down the Alt key.

FIGURE 3.7

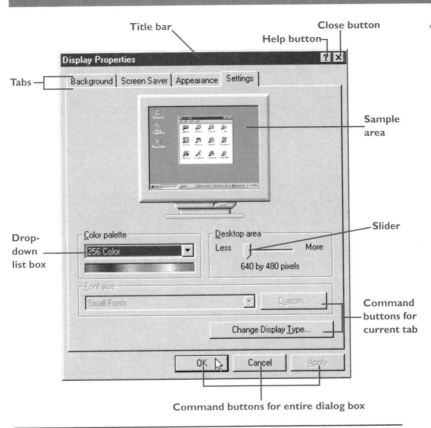

Title bar

Help button

Close button

Tabs

Drop-down list box

Sample area

Slider

Command buttons for current tab

Command buttons for entire dialog box

A typical dialog box and its controls

Common Types of Controls

Now, let's take a quick look at some common types of controls, what they do, and how you use them. Once you've mastered Controls 101, you should have no trouble working anything in Windows.

Check Box This control lets you select an item independently of any other check boxes. A ✔ or × appears in the box when it is selected (or *on*); the box is empty when it is deselected

We've listed these controls in alphabetical order.

(or *off*). To turn the check box on or off, click on the check box, or move to the check box and press the Spacebar, or press Alt+*letter*.

Column Heading   This describes information that appears in a column. You can drag the vertical divider between columns to make the column narrower or wider, or double-click on the divider to make the text fit snugly within the column. To sort by a particular column, click on the column heading (click again to undo the sort).

Name	Size	Type	Modified
Microsof	3KB	Microsoft Program Gr...	6/8/95 4:06 PM
Midimap.std	36KB	STD File	8/24/94 1:34 AM
Midimap.vst	19KB	VST File	9/9/94 11:52 AM
Mktmsgr	1KB	Configuration Settings	2/9/95 12:25 PM
Monitors	28KB	Configuration Settings	1/21/95 4:48 PM

Combo Box   This lets you select information from a list box (see below) or type data into a text box (see below).

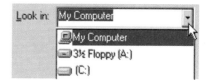

Command Button This control carries out the related command. To

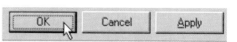

activate the button, click on it, or move to it and press ↵, or press Alt+*letter*. Many dialog boxes contain an OK button, a Cancel button, and sometimes an Apply button. Choosing OK accepts your changes and closes the dialog box. Choosing Cancel (or pressing Esc) discards your changes and closes the dialog box. Choosing Apply shows the effects of your changes and commits those changes. For example, if you choose Apply, make some more changes, and then choose Cancel, the changes you made before choosing Apply are saved and the changes you make after choosing Apply are ignored.

The command buttons at the bottom of a dialog box apply to the entire dialog box.

List Box This lets you choose an item from a list. If the list isn't visible, it's called a drop-down list (or pick list). To open a drop-down list, click on the ▼ button next to the list or 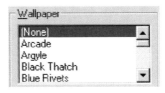 move to the list box and press Alt+↓. To select an option from an opened list, click on the option or highlight it with the arrow keys on your keyboard and then press ↵.

To quickly highlight an item in a list, type the first letter or letters of the item.

Option Button (or Radio Button) This control lets you select one option in a group  (selecting an option button is like choosing a station on your car radio). Only one option can be selected within the group. To select an option button,

- Click on it, or

- Move to the group and press an arrow key until the correct option is highlighted, or

- Press Alt+*letter*.

Slider This lets you adjust continuous values such as volume, speed, or brightness. To 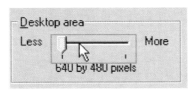 use a slider, drag the indicator along the slider bar or move to the slider option and press the arrow keys as needed.

Spin Box This control lets you cycle through values. Click on the ↑ or ↓ arrow button to increase or decrease the value, or move to the spin box and press the ↑ or ↓ keys on your keyboard, or type a value into the text box.

Tab This lets you switch to a different *page*

of options in a dialog box. To select a tab, click on it or move to the current tab and press the arrow keys on your keyboard to highlight the tab you want.

There's more info on typing and editing text in Chapter 6.

Text Box   This lets you supply information by typing text. To enter text, click in the text box, move to the text box, or press Alt+*letter*. Then start typing. Here are some quick tips for working with text:

Share **N**ame: MY TOOLS

- If you make a mistake, press the Backspace or Delete key to delete text to the left or right of the insertion point, respectively.

- To position the insertion point within the text, click the mouse where you want the insertion point to appear or press the ← and → keys on your keyboard.

- If the text is selected (highlighted) within the text box, just start typing; you will completely replace the high-lighted text.

- To select text, drag the mouse pointer through the text or position the insertion point and then hold down the Shift key while pressing ← or → as needed.

Using Toolbars

If you're not sure what a toolbar control is for, just point to it with your mouse and wait until the handy pop-up description appears.

Many windows offer *toolbars*, which provide shortcut alternatives to menus. Figure 3.8 shows the toolbar for a window that displays files and folders. If the toolbar isn't visible, choose <u>V</u>iew ➤ <u>T</u>oolbar from the window's menu bar. (Choosing <u>V</u>iew ➤ <u>T</u>oolbar once more will hide the toolbar again.)

Toolbar controls work a lot like the ones in dialog boxes. For example, to activate a button, just click on it. To use a drop-down list, click on the button beside the list and then click on the item you want.

FIGURE 3.8

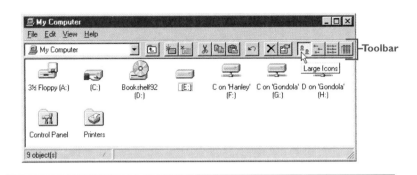

A toolbar for a window that displays files and folders

CHAPTER 4

Managing Files, Folders, and Objects

Featuring

- What is a file?
- What is a folder?
- Finding, selecting, and manipulating objects
- Creating new files and folders

When you walk into a room, you see a bunch of *objects:* chairs, tables, lamps, books, loose change, and so forth. Your computer is full of objects too. And just as you can manipulate day-to-day objects, moving them around and even changing their appearance, you can manipulate the objects in your computer.

The two main types of objects that you'll manipulate are *folders* and *files*. If you took the hands-on tutorial mentioned in Chapter 2, you've already had a little experience with these objects. In this chapter, we're going to round out your object-manipulation skills so you can take control of the computer and make it do what *you* want it to do. We'll start with a general discussion of the two main types of objects: the file and the folder.

What Is a File?

A *file* is a single unit of information stored on a computer disk. These files can contain basically *anything* that can be put into digital form—including written text, pictures, sound, and movies (video), just to name a few. There are three *types* of information a file can store:

Program (or *application*) A file can contain instructions that the computer (not people) can "read" to make it behave a certain way. *Examples:* WordPerfect, Lotus 1-2-3, and others introduced back in Table 1.1 of Chapter 1.

Msaccess.exe

Documents A file can contain any information that you, or any other computer user, create. *Examples:* Written text (letters, memos, book chapters), pictures, sound, movies (video), and so on.

Orders.mdb

Document and data icons usually resemble a dog-eared piece of paper. The icon inside the paper represents the program that was used to create that document.

Program Data A program's data files contain information that a computer guru can modify to change the way a program behaves. *Examples:* The file named Win.ini

Autoexec.dos

(for *Windows initialization*) contains information that Windows uses at start-up to get situated on your particular PC. In general, you don't need to mess with data files directly.

What Is a Folder?

Folders are similar to the manila folders in a filing cabinet. Like manila folders, the folders on your computer are used to keep related items together in one convenient spot. A folder can contain all types of files, as well as other folders.

Sampapps

You ex-DOS/Windows users may recognize that a folder is what we used to call a directory.

Three Steps for Managing Any Object

Whenever you need to do something with (or to) an object (be it a file, folder, or whatever), you'll go through this basic three-step procedure:

- First, *find* the object you want.

- Second, *select* the object or objects you want to work with.

- Third, *do* whatever it is you want to do with that object.

We'll discuss how you do each of those steps in the three sections that follow.

Step 1: Finding the Object

There are many different ways to find an object on your computer. The best method depends on what you already know about the object, as summarized below.

- If there's an icon for the object on the desktop or in the taskbar, there's no need to look any further. You've already found the object and can skip right to *Step 2: Selecting the Object* later in this chapter.

Don't be intimidated by the fact that there are umpteen different ways to do things. Remember, there's no "right way" or "wrong way." Just use whatever method seems most convenient at the moment.

● If you've used the object recently, but don't see an icon for it on the screen, you may be able to reopen it simply by choosing Start ➤ Documents. If you see the object in the menu that appears, you're ready to move on. Just skip to *Step 2: Selecting the Object* later in this chapter.

● If you know the name of the object—or even part of the name—but don't see an icon for it on the screen or in the Documents menu, you can use the Find feature to find the object. See the next section, *Finding a File or Folder by Name*.

● If you don't know the name of the object you want, or you just want to go exploring to see what's available on this PC, see *Browsing Around* later in this chapter.

Finding a File or Folder by Name

If you know all or part of the name of the object you're looking for, you can use the Find feature to track it down. Here's how:

① Choose Start ➤ Find ➤ Files or Folders (or just right-click on the Start button and choose Find).

② If it's not already selected, click on the Name & Location tab in the dialog box (see Figure 4.1).

③ In the Named text box, type any part of the name you're searching for or click on the ▼ button and pick a previously used name from the drop-down list.

④ Make sure the *Look in* text box shows the place you want to look for folders and files. If it doesn't, click on the drop-down button next to *Look in* and pick a place. Alternatively, click on the Browse button and double-click on an icon or folder until you find the place you want to begin; then click on OK.

⑤ If you don't want to search through folders that are below the place in the *Look in* text box, deselect *Include subfolders*.

You also can search for files based on their Date Modified, and you can do Advanced searches based on file contents or size. Just click on the Date Modified or Advanced tab and fill in the dialog box that appears.

FIGURE 4.1

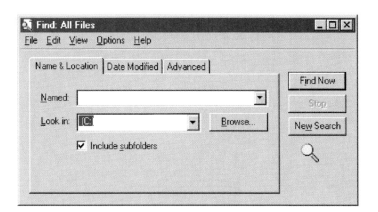

The Find: All Files dialog box lets you search for files or folders by name.

6 Click on F<u>i</u>nd Now and wait patiently until the matching names appear. If no matches were found, you can click on Ne<u>w</u> Search to clear the current search, then choose OK and return to step 1, above.

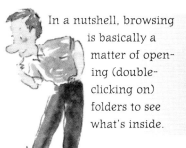

If a search seems to be taking too long, or if you change your mind about doing a particular search, you can just click on Stop to stop searching.

Assuming your search was successful, the Find dialog box will look something like Figure 4.2.

Here are two things you can do once the file and folder names appear:

● To open a folder, double-click on it.

● To sort the list of files and folders by any of the column headings, click on the appropriate column heading. To return to the previous sort order, click on the column heading again.

Browsing Around

Browsing is handy when you just want to look around and see what's available or when you're looking for something but aren't sure of its exact name.

In a nutshell, browsing is basically a matter of opening (double-clicking on) folders to see what's inside.

FIGURE 4.2

The Find dialog box after a successful search

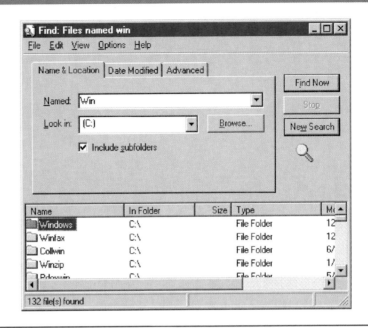

Browsing with My Computer If you want to browse around your own computer (as opposed to other computers you might be connected to), follow these steps:

❶ Double-click on the *My Computer* icon on your desktop. This opens a window, similar to Figure 4.3.

❷ Double-click on the icon for the drive you want to search. You'll see a window full of folders and files similar to Figure 4.4.

❸ From here, just double-click your way through the folders until you get to the folder that contains the files (or folders) you're looking for. The upper-left corner of the title bar will indicate which drive or folder you're viewing at the moment.

FIGURE 4.3

Double-click on My Computer to browse your computer...

...then double-click on a drive icon to browse that drive

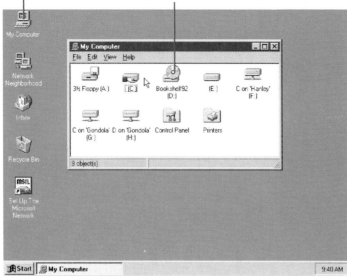

My Computer window opened on the desktop

FIGURE 4.4

Double-click on any folder to see what's inside

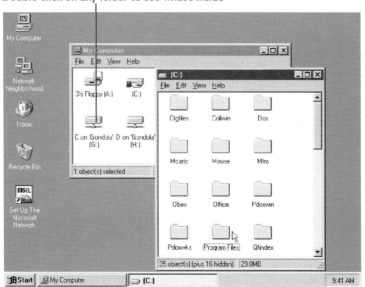

The desktop after double-clicking on the icon for drive C (the hard disk inside your computer)

Here are two quick tips for controlling the appearance and behavior of browsing windows that display lists of files and folders:

● If the window doesn't show a toolbar or status bar, choose View ➤ Toolbar or View ➤ Status Bar as needed.

To find a computer on your net-work and then search through its folders and files, choose Start ➤ Find ➤ Computer, then type the name of the computer you're searching for and click on Find Now. You can then double-click on the com-puter's icon and pro-ceed through the folders.

● To prevent a new window from opening each time you double-click on a folder or drive icon, choose View ➤ Options, then click on the Folder tab and click on *Browse folders by using a single window that changes as you open each folder*. Click on OK.

Browsing with Network Neighborhood   If your computer is attached to other computers via a local-area network (LAN), you can use the Network Neighborhood icon to browse around the connected computers.

Here's how:

1   Double-click on the icon *Network Neighborhood* on the desktop. A list of computers in your *workgroup* appears in the Network Neighborhood window.

2   To see the *shared folders* on a particular computer, double-click on the name of the computer. Figure 4.5 shows an example where we've opened Network Neighborhood, then double-clicked on the name of one of the computers in our workgroup. (We also chose View ➤ Details within each window to see more infor-mation about each shared item.)

A *workgroup* is a collection of computers that are linked together to share printers and files. Any member of a workgroup can *share* a folder located on his or her PC, so other work-group members can use the files in that folder. We'll talk about local-area networks in Chapter 12.

3   Now just double-click your way through the folders as usual until you locate the folder or file you're look-ing for.

Remember that every time you double-click on something, you're opening it up into a window. If you double-click on a folder icon, the next window to appear will show you the con-tents of that folder. If you double-click on a file's icon, the next window to appear will show you the contents of that one file.

FIGURE 4.5

Double-click on Network Neighborhood to browse your network
Double-click on a computer icon to browse that computer
Double-click on a drive folder to browse that drive

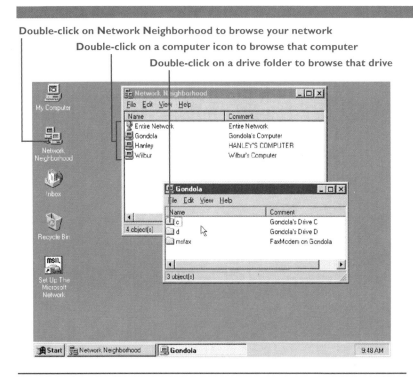

The desktop after double-clicking on Network Neighborhood, then double-clicking on the icon for one of the computers in the workgroup.

Either way, you can back up and close the window you just opened by clicking on the Close button (X) in the upper-right corner of that window.

Browsing with Windows Explorer Windows Explorer offers yet another way to browse around your computer and the local network. It's something like My Computer and Network Neighborhood rolled into one, except that it shows you everything in a neat treelike structure that doesn't clutter the screen. Here's how to use Explorer:

Also, remember that to tidy up all the open windows on your desktop in a jiffy, you can just right-click on some blank part of the taskbar. Then choose Cascade from the pop-up menu that appears.

1 Choose Start ➤ Programs ➤ Windows Explorer or right-click on the Start button, any folder, or drive icon and choose Explore from the pop-up menu. An Exploring window similar to the one in Figure 4.6 will appear on the desktop.

Explorer combines features of My Computer and Network Neighborhood in one convenient place. In this example, we chose View ➤ Details and View ➤ Toolbar.

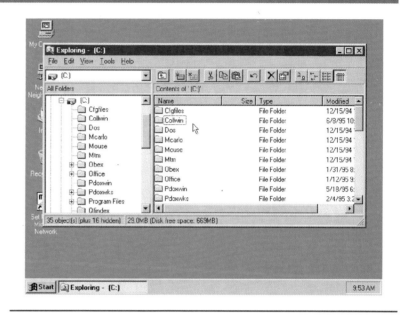

If you're an experienced Windows user, the Windows Explorer will be the most familiar tool you have for browsing around and managing files. Microsoft describes the Windows Explorer as "the File Manager on steroids." If you want Explorer to look more like File Manager, choose View ➤ Details or View ➤ List from the Exploring menu bar.

2 Here are some techniques you can use to navigate with Explorer:

- To switch your view to another computer, disk drive, or folder, click on the appropriate icon in the *left* side of the window. If you selected a folder, that folder will appear opened in the left side of the window. The right side of the window will reflect the contents of whatever icon you clicked on.

- If an icon is marked with a plus sign (+) in the *left* side of the window, click on that plus sign to expand the icon; it will show another level down. The plus sign will change to a minus sign (−). To collapse the icon and hide its lower levels, click on the minus sign.

- To open a folder in the *right* side of the window, double-click on the folder. The contents of the right side of the window will change accordingly.

- To quickly bounce your view of files, folders, and icons one level higher, simply press the Backspace key or click the Up One Level button in the tool-bar (if it's visible).

Windows Explorer gives you a lot of control over the appearance and alphabetical order of names in any browse window. We'll turn to these topics next.

Changing Your Point of View As you're browsing through folders and windows, you can look at the information in the current window in a variety of ways:

- Click on <u>V</u>iew from the menu bar or right-click on an empty spot in the right section of the window or desktop and choose <u>V</u>iew. Then click on Large Icons, S<u>m</u>all Icons, <u>L</u>ist, or <u>D</u>etails.

- Or click on the Large Icons, Small Icons, List, or Details buttons in any toolbar that offers them (back in Figure 4.6 these are the four rightmost buttons in the toolbar).

Sorting the icons is just as easy. First click on the <u>V</u>iew menu in the menu bar or right-click on an empty spot in the window or desktop. Then click on Arrange <u>I</u>cons and click on the sorting option you want (for example, by <u>N</u>ame, by <u>T</u>ype, by Si<u>z</u>e, or by <u>D</u>ate).

To align the icons neatly on an invisible grid, click on <u>V</u>iew in the menu bar or right-click on an empty spot in the window or desktop, then choose Line up Icon<u>s</u>. If you'd like the icons to stay lined up even if you drag them around, click on <u>V</u>iew in the menu bar or right-click on an empty spot in the window or desktop. Next click on Arrange <u>I</u>cons and select (check) <u>A</u>uto Arrange.

This trick of bouncing up one level works in any window that displays folders and files. Try it in the My Computer or Network Neighborhood windows when you get a chance!

Confused by the various views? Just keep in mind that changing the view or sort order doesn't change the *content* of the window you're in. Rather, you're just changing the *way* of looking at that information. Use whichever view and sort order is most convenient at the moment.

In the real world, you usually need to get your hands on an object before you can do something with it. *Selecting* an object on the screen is roughly the equivalent of getting your hands on an object in the real world.

The *exact* selection techniques you can use at any moment vary. For example, you *can't* drag a marquee around a hierarchical list of folder names in the left side of the Exploring window. If a particular method doesn't work in the context you're in at the moment, just try one of the other methods.

Step 2: Selecting the Object

Once you've found an object's icon, you may need to *select* it before doing something with it. You can tell when an object is selected by its appearance. Typically, the selected object will be

C on 'Gondola' (G:)   D on 'Gondola' (H:)   Control Panel   Printers

colored differently and its label (name) shown with light letters against a dark background. For example, here the Control Panel folder is the selected object.

Here's how you can select one or more objects on your screen:

- To select one object, just click on it or press the arrow keys on your keyboard until you highlight the object you want.

- To select more than one object, hold down the Ctrl key while clicking on each object (this is called *Ctrl+clicking*).

- To select several objects that are next to one another, move your mouse pointer to just outside one of the objects. Then hold down the mouse button and drag an outline (also called a *marquee*) around the objects you want to select. As you drag, the objects will be highlighted.

- In many cases, you can select all the objects within a window. To do so, choose Edit ➤ Select All from that window's menu bar or press Ctrl+A.

Of course, you might occasionally select something by accident. No big deal. You can just as easily deselect an object:

- To deselect an object, or all the selected objects, click on some neutral area away from the objects (or select a different object).

- To deselect one of several selected objects, Ctrl+click on the object you want to deselect.

● To invert the current selection in the window, choose
Edit ➤ Invert Selection from the menu bar.

To *invert* a selection
means to change the
selected objects to
the unselected
objects and the un-
selected objects to the
selected objects.

You also can select an object by right-clicking on it. As mentioned, right-clicking has the added bonus of displaying an
instant pop-up menu of things you can do right on the spot
with the selected object.

Now that you know how to find objects on your computer
and how to select them, we can focus on all the great stuff you
can do with these objects.

Step 3: Manipulating the Object

Once you've found and selected an object, there are a lot of
things you can do with it.

To broaden your knowledge of the possibilities, Table 4.1 lists
the most common actions that you'll perform on objects—particularly on files and folders. We'll discuss in more detail how
to perform each of those actions in the sections that follow.

TABLE 4.1

*Common Operations
Allowed on Files and
Folders*

Operation	What It Does
Copy	Copies the folder or file to the Windows Clipboard
Create Shortcut	Makes a desktop icon that provides quick entry to the folder or file
Cut	Moves the folder or file to the Windows Clipboard
Delete	Deletes the file or folder and (usually) puts it in the Recycle Bin
Edit	Opens a file so you can view and/or change its content
Explore	Opens a folder (not a file) inside the Windows Explorer

TABLE 4.1

Common Operations Allowed on Files and Folders (continued)

Operation	What It Does
Find	Searches the current folder for a particular file
Open	Displays the contents of the folder or file on your screen
Open With	Opens a document file (not a folder) using whatever program you specify
Paste	Copies whatever is in the Windows Clipboard to the currently selected folder
Print	Prints the contents of a document (or data) file on paper (see Chapter 5)
Properties	Displays and lets you change various characteristics of the object
Quick View	Displays the contents of the file on the screen for viewing only
Rename	Changes the name of a file or folder
Send To	Sends the file to a disk or to a fax recipient
Sharing	Lets other people on a network have access to the selected folder and all the files within it (see Chapter 13)

Keep in mind that always, always, always, the fastest and easiest way to do something with an object is just to right-click on it and then choose an option from the pop-up menu that appears.

Copying and Moving Objects

Often you'll want to copy an object from one place to another or move an object to a different spot. For instance, you might want to copy some files from drive C (your hard disk) to a floppy disk in drive A. You could then keep the floppy disk as backup for the original files, mail it to someone, or copy it to the hard disk on your home or office computer.

When you *copy* an object, you make an exact duplicate of it. One copy exists in the original spot and another exists in a new spot. When you *move* an object, you delete the object from its original place and copy it to a new place (ending up with just one object).

Some Things Shouldn't Be Moved (or Deleted)!

Before you get too excited about moving things all over creation, be aware that moving can get you into trouble. Why? Because most programs expect their supporting data files to be in a certain place. If you move them somewhere else (or worse, delete them), the program may not work anymore. So be careful not to move anything that another program (or person) expects to be in a certain location. If you move something accidentally, simply move it back to its original location. If you're not sure where you moved it, use Start ➤ Find ➤ Files or Folders to find it again; then move it back to the proper place.

Copying and Moving with the Clipboard　The Windows *Clipboard* is a place in the computer's memory that can store one object or one piece of information temporarily. This information can be just about anything you want—a chunk of text, a file or folder, a picture or sound clip, whatever. Once the information is on the Clipboard, you can paste it anywhere you want.

Here's how to use the Clipboard to move or copy a file or folder object:

Anything you put in the Clipboard stays there until you either put something else on the Clipboard or shut down Windows.

❶　Find and select the object(s) you want to move or copy.

To see what's on the Clipboard at any time, open WordPad and choose Edit ➤ Paste. Or, if you've installed the Clipboard Viewer accessory, click on Start, then choose Programs ➤ Accessories Clipboard ➤ Viewer.

2 Put the object on the Clipboard using one of the methods below:

- To *copy* the object, choose Edit ➤ Copy from the menu bar, or press Ctrl+C, or right-click on the object and choose Copy. The object will be placed on the Clipboard, and the original object will stay where it is.

- To *move* the object, choose Edit ➤ Cut, or press Ctrl+X, or right-click on the object and choose Cut. The original object will be placed on the Clipboard, and it will disappear from its original place.

3 Select the object that you want to copy/move the Clipboard's contents to. (If you want to put the contents in an open folder's window, click on the open folder's title bar—not on a folder within the window.)

4 Choose Edit ➤ Paste from the menu bar, or press Ctrl+V, or right-click and choose Paste.

The Clipboard Is a Universal Thing

The Clipboard can be used to move or copy just about anything—not just files or folders, but also text, sound clips, movies, graphics, whatever! For example, you can use the Clipboard to copy or move information from one part of a document to another or from one application to another. The basic steps for using the Clipboard are always the same. First, *select* the information you want to copy or move. Next, *copy* or *cut* the selected information to the Clipboard. Finally, go to the place where the information should appear and *paste* the Clipboard contents to the new location.

Copying and Moving with Drag and Drop If you don't want to use the Clipboard, you can use drag and drop to copy or move. Here's how:

1 Find and select the object you want to copy or move.

2 Make sure you can also see the object (e.g., folder) that you want to move/copy your selection to.

- If you want to **copy** the object, hold down the Ctrl key and drag the object to the destination.

- If you want to **move** the object, hold down the Alt key and drag the object to its new destination.

To easily memorize the Copy shortcut, remember that both Copy and Ctrl start with the letter *C*.

If You Just Drag... You can also just drag the object from one place to another without holding down either key. When you do, Windows 95 will do the following:

- If you drag the object to another folder on the same drive, Windows 95 will *move* the object to that folder.

- If you drag the object to a folder on a different drive, Windows 95 will *copy* the object to that folder. A small + sign will appear near the ghost image of the object you're dragging to indicate that you're *adding* a copy of the object to the new destination.

Right-Dragging Yet a third way to move or copy an object is to *right-drag* the object:

1 Right-drag (hold down the *secondary* mouse button) the object to its new location, then release the mouse button.

2 In the pop-up menu that appears, click on either <u>M</u>ove Here (to move) or <u>C</u>opy Here (to copy).

Renaming Objects

Sometimes you might want to change the name of an object, perhaps because you mistyped it the first time or just because you've thought up a better name. To change the name of an object:

1 Find the object you want to rename.

2 Right-click on the object and choose Rename, or choose <u>F</u>ile ➤ Rena<u>m</u>e from the menu bar, or simply click on the name that you want to change. A box will appear around the object's name and the entire name will be selected (highlighted).

3 Now you can use the standard Windows text-editing techniques summarized below to change the current name:

● To completely replace the current name, just type the new name.

● To change the existing name, first position the blinking insertion point where you want to make a change. Just click where you want to make the change or use the Home, End, ←, or → keys to position the insertion point. Then type in new text and/or press Delete (Del) or Backspace to delete existing text.

A good general rule to keep in mind: when text is selected, anything you type will instantly replace all the selected text. To just modify the selected text, press an arrow key, Home, or End— or click where you want to make a change—to move the insertion point before you type a character.

Opening Objects

The most common thing to do with a file is to *open* it. What happens when you open the file depends, of course, on what kind of information the file contains. For example, if it contains a word-processing *program* such as WordPad or Microsoft Word, that program will run. If it contains a word-processing *document*, the word-processing program will run *and* your document will open in the window.

The easiest way to open a file is to double-click on it in any browse window or on the desktop. You also can select one or more files, then right-click and choose <u>O</u>pen from the property sheet; or you can select the file(s) and choose File ➤ Open from the menu bar.

Using Open With Windows normally uses the file's extension to decide which program to use when you double-click on a document file. If Windows can't figure out which program to use, it displays the Open With dialog box shown in Figure 4.7. (This same dialog box appears if you right-click on the file and choose Open With or you select it and choose File ➤ Open With.)

To choose a program from the Open With list, simply scroll through the list and click on the name of the program you used to create the file. If you can't find that program in the list, click on the Other button, search through the computer or network for the program you need, then double-click on the program's name. Choose OK to launch the program and open the document.

You rarely see the file-name extension in Windows 95, so its ability to open the appropriate program might seem like magic. For example, even if you save a Word document with the name Letter to Grandma, it will actually be saved as Letter to Grandma.doc. But you'll only see the .doc if you choose View ➤ Options (in any My Computer or Exploring window), click on the View tab, and select the *Hide MS-DOS file extensions...* option.

FIGURE 4.7

Use the Open With dialog box to find a program to use for opening the selected file.

If you did a Typical install, Quick View might not be set up (Chapter 10 explains how to install new programs). Note that Quick View works for registered file types only (and only if an appropriate viewer is available). Adding a registered file type is covered in *Creating and Changing Associations* in Chapter 5.

Quick-Viewing a File   Sometimes you'll just want to take a quick peek at a document without bothering to launch the program that created it. To do that, select one or more files. Then right-click and choose Quick View, or choose File ➤ Quick View from the menu bar. Here are some handy things you can do next:

- To launch the program so you can edit the document, choose File ➤ Open File for Editing or click on the Open File for Editing button at the left edge of the toolbar.

- To display a full-page view of the document, choose View ➤ Page View from the menu bar. Figure 4.8 illustrates a graphics file in the Quick View window after

FIGURE 4.8

A graphic in the Quick View window in Page View

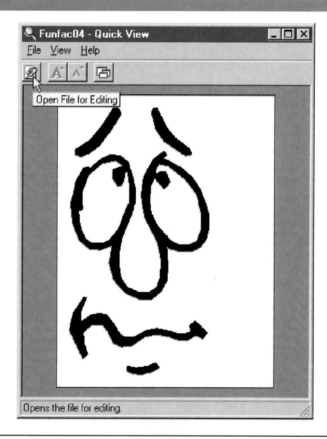

zooming the window to Page View. Choose <u>V</u>iew ➤
<u>P</u>age View again to return to normal full-size view.

Deleting Objects

When you no longer need an object, you can delete it. Because
deleting files and folders is a pretty final thing, Windows provides
a built-in safety net—called the *Recycle Bin*—on your desktop.

Deleted objects remain in the Recycle Bin until you empty the
bin (much as the trash you recycle remains in your recycling bin
until you dump it).

Some deleted objects can't be put in the Recycle Bin. If
Windows can't recycle something you're about to delete, it will
let you know and give you a chance to change your mind.
Think before you make your choice!

Even though the Recycle Bin can save your hide if you delete
something accidentally, you still need to be very careful about
deleting objects on your computer. *Never* delete a data file that
a program needs, *never* delete a program that someone is
using, and *never* delete shared folders on a network. If you do
delete something accidentally, you should retrieve it from the
Recycle Bin as soon as possible (as explained later).

Deleting
a folder
will
delete the
folder and
all the files and
folders it contains!
Windows 3.1
users beware:
Unlike
version 3.1,
deleting an icon in Windows 95
does delete the underlying files!

By the way, you'll always know whether the Recycle Bin is
empty or not. When it's empty, it looks like this:

And when it's not empty, it contains crumpled papers, like this:

Follow these steps to delete objects and put them into the Recycle Bin:

1 Find and select the object(s) you want to delete.

2 Do one of the following:

- Drag and drop the object(s) onto the Recycle Bin icon.

- Press the Delete key, or right-click on the object(s) and choose Delete, or choose File ➤ Delete from the menu bar.

3 If you're asked whether you're sure you want to delete the object(s), choose Yes (if you're sure) or No (if you've changed your mind).

When we get to Chapter 5, we'll discuss *shortcuts*. But just to let you know, you *can* delete a shortcut icon at any time without deleting the actual files that the icon represents.

Using the Recycle Bin   You can use the Recycle Bin to get deleted objects back again (undelete them) or to delete objects permanently. To open the Recycle Bin, double-click on it as you would any icon. Figure 4.9 shows a Recycle Bin window that contains several (temporarily) deleted objects.

The Recycle Bin window works like most others that show files and folders. However, some special things you can do with it are listed below:

- To undelete objects and restore them to their original locations, select the object(s). Then right-click and choose Restore or choose File ➤ Restore from the menu bar.

- To undelete objects and put them wherever you want them, select the object(s). Then find the place where you want them to reappear and drag them to the appropriate spot.

The Recycle Bin retains its files even after you shut down Windows 95 and turn off your computer. The files in the Recycle Bin continue to consume disk space until you specifically empty the Recycle Bin!

FIGURE 4.9

Name	Original Location	Date Deleted	Type	Size
ART3.WMF	C:\Old Stuff	6/9/95 11:57 AM	WMF File	8KB
ART4.WMF	C:\Old Stuff	6/9/95 11:57 AM	WMF File	8KB
ART5.WMF	C:\Old Stuff	6/9/95 11:57 AM	WMF File	15KB
ART6.WMF	C:\Old Stuff	6/9/95 11:57 AM	WMF File	9KB
ART7.WMF	C:\Old Stuff	6/9/95 11:57 AM	WMF File	20KB
QP.WMF	C:\Old Stuff	6/9/95 11:57 AM	WMF File	137KB
TEST.QDI	C:\Old Stuff	6/9/95 11:57 AM	QDI File	1KB
TEST.QDT	C:\Old Stuff	6/9/95 11:57 AM	QDT File	2KB
TEST.QMT	C:\Old Stuff	6/9/95 11:57 AM	QMT File	4KB

9 object(s) — 199KB

The Recycle Bin opened on the desktop

- To permanently delete objects from the Recycle Bin and the disk, select the object(s). Then right-click and choose <u>D</u>elete, or click on the Delete button in the toolbar, or choose <u>F</u>ile ➤ <u>D</u>elete from the menu bar. Choose <u>Y</u>es to finish the job.

- To permanently delete all the objects in one fell swoop, right-click on the Recycle Bin icon on the desktop and choose Empty Recycle <u>B</u>in from the property menu or choose <u>F</u>ile ➤ Empty Recycle <u>B</u>in from the Recycle Bin window's menu bar. Choose <u>Y</u>es to confirm the deed.

- To restore the most recently deleted objects from the Recycle Bin to their original locations, choose <u>E</u>dit ➤ <u>U</u>ndo Delete from the menu bar or click on the Undo Delete button in the toolbar.

Creating Folders

As you've seen, folders are handy for organizing icons (including files and other folders) into related groups. You can create new folders anytime you want to reorganize things on your desktop. Here's how:

1 Go to the window that should contain the new folder or click on the desktop if you want to create a folder

It's never necessary to create new folders to reorganize programs and their related files. All programs that you install will set up their own folders automatically. All this business of creating new folders is strictly optional.

there. (In a moment, we'll show you an example of creating a folder within a folder.)

2 Right-click on an empty area in the window or desktop and choose Ne<u>w</u> ➤ <u>F</u>older from the property sheet, or choose <u>F</u>ile ➤ <u>N</u>ew ➤ <u>F</u>older from the menu bar. A new folder icon appears, and the name *New Folder* is highlighted just below the icon.

3 Type a new name for the folder and press ↵.

No two folders within a folder can have the same name. So make sure that when typing in the name for your new folder, you don't use a name that's already been used.

Let's suppose you want to put a new folder named *Budgets* inside another new folder named *1995 Business Records* on disk drive C.

To begin, double-click on *My Computer* on the desktop, then double-click on the drive C icon. Choose <u>F</u>ile ➤ <u>N</u>ew ➤ <u>F</u>older, type **1995 Business Records**, and press ↵. Next double-click on the icon for 1995 Business Records to open this folder (initially the folder will be empty). Now, to place the Budgets folder inside the 1995 Business Records folder, choose <u>F</u>ile ➤ <u>N</u>ew ➤ <u>F</u>older, type **Budgets**, and press ↵. Using a typical analogy from the world of business, you can think of this folder-within-a-folder business as sliding a manila folder named Budgets inside a manila folder named 1995 Business Records and then putting both folders into a file drawer labeled Drive C.

Once you've created a folder, you can move or copy files and folders into it as explained a bit later.

File and Folder Names

You might think of the folder and file names as labels on manila file folders. Their purpose is to tell you what's inside the folder so you don't have to open it to find out.

You'll want to give your folders and files meaningful names to help you identify what's inside without having to open them.

Basically, a file or folder name can be whatever pops into your head. There are a few minor rules and facts, however, that you need to keep in mind:

- The name can be no more than 255 characters in length.

- The name can contain letters, spaces, numbers, and any of these punctuation characters:

  & ' @ , $ = !

  ` - { } ( ) [ ]

  # ` ' % + ; ~ _

- Each folder on a particular disk must have a unique name. For example, you can't have two folders both named My Goodies, though you could have a folder named My Goodies 1 and My Goodies 2.

- Each file within a folder must have a unique name. For example, a folder named Windows 95 Book could *not* contain two files named Chapter 1. But it *could* contain files named Chapter 1, Chapter 2, Chapter 3, and so forth.

- Windows will keep whatever uppercase and lowercase letters you type, but it does not discriminate based on upper- or lowercase. For example, to Windows, the file names MY STUFF, my stuff, My stuff, and My Stuff are all the same.

- Blank spaces *do* count. For example, the name MyStuff is *not* the same as My Stuff (which contains a space.)

- Spaces at the beginning or end of a file name are stripped off automatically.

DOS and Windows 3.1 programs can't display all 255 characters. So try to make the first few characters in the folder or file name count. For example, if you name a folder Projects from Ashley's FutureKids Class and name another Projects from Alec's Daycare center, those names will appear as PROJEC~1 and PROJEC~2 in DOS/Windows applications. Better to use names like Ashley FutureKids Projects and Alec Daycare Projects, which will be shortened to ALECDA~1 and ASHLEY~1. Not great names, but better than the other alternative.

Sometimes Only Eight Characters Will Work

Windows 95 files still use a three-character extension, but that extension is often hidden. Nonetheless, the extension plays an important role, as we'll discuss in the next chapter.

If you've been using PCs for a while, you'll no doubt appreciate the new 255-character file names. It's a *big* improvement over the old "8.3" limit imposed by DOS and Windows 3.1. The 8.3 refers to the fact that the file name can be no more than eight characters in length, followed by a period (dot) and up to a three-letter extension.

Unfortunately, the 8.3 rule still does apply in many situations. For example, if you're using a DOS program, or a program written for Windows 3.1, that particular program will still only allow 8.3-style names. The only way around that will be to upgrade to the Windows 95 (or 32-bit, as it may be called) version of the program.

CHAPTER 5

Using Your Programs

Featuring

- How to start a program
- Using a program
- Creating shortcuts to frequently used programs
- Autostarting favorite programs
- A trick way to print documents
- How to open a document

As you may recall from earlier chapters, a *program* is something you generally purchase from a computer store and install on your PC. A *document* is something that you create using whatever program you have that's best suited for creating that type of document. The document can be something you type or draw, a photograph, recorded sound—whatever.

In this chapter we'll take a look at general techniques for starting, using, and exiting programs that are currently installed on your PC.

Chapters 6 and 7 show some specific examples of programs and documents using programs that came with your Windows 95 package.

How to Start a Program

There are a lot of ways to start any program on your PC. We'll summarize the various techniques below, starting with the simplest method and working toward the more complex:

1 To start a program, try each method below until you find the one that works for you.

● Take a look at the taskbar and, if you see an icon for the program you want to start,

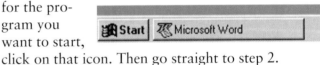

click on that icon. Then go straight to step 2.

● If you see an icon for the program on your desktop, then double-click on that icon and go to step 2.

● If you have a suite of programs, like Microsoft Office, and you can see the toolbar for that suite, click on the button for the program you want to start. Then skip to step 2.

If you want to restart a program and also reopen a document you saved recently, try choosing Start ➤ Documents. If you see the name of the document you want to reopen, just click on its name. The program will start and automatically open your document for you!

● Click on the Start button and choose <u>P</u>rograms. If the program you want to start is in the menu, click on its icon. Otherwise, click on the name of the folder that contains the program you want to start until you find the program's icon. *Then* click on the icon for the program you want to start (see Figure 5.1). Then go to step 2.

● If all of the above fail, try using <u>F</u>ind to locate the program (see Chapter 4). Then go to step 2.

FIGURE 5.1

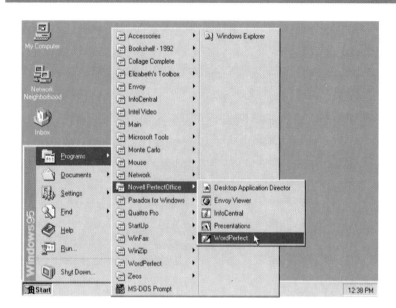

Opening Novell Perfect Office

To start a program that has no icon on the desktop, choose Start ➤ Programs, then point to the appropriate folder(s) until you find the icon for the program you want to start.

- If you just want to browse around and see what programs are available on your system, use the Browse technique described in Chapter 4.

- If you know the exact location and name of the program but cannot find its icon, click on the Start button and choose Run. Type the location and file name of the program you want to start. Alternatively, choose Browse and work your way through the folders until you find an icon for the program you want to start. Then double-click on the program's icon and choose OK.

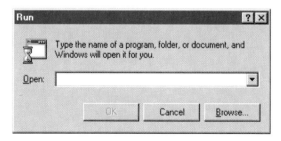

2 The program will start in its own window, as in the example shown in Figure 5.2.

FIGURE 5.2

Any program you start will appear in its own window. In most cases, that window will have the various features and controls pointed out here. (This is the window for a program called WordPerfect.)

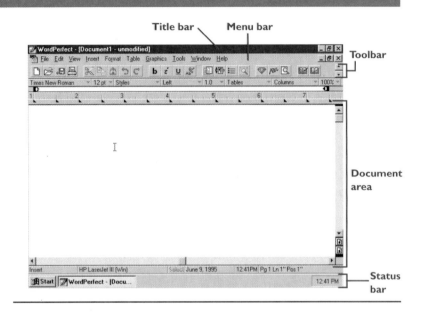

Some programs will automatically display an optional tutorial for beginners— or a "Tip of the Day" for more experienced users— when your program first opens. Just follow the instructions that appear within that smaller window to explore your options.

Tools That Most Programs Provide

Every program you use will have its own set of instructions, usually both in paper form (a User's Guide that comes with the program) and online documentation (built-in help). But most programs share certain characteristics and features that you can start using right away, even before you read the instructions. Those common features include:

- A **title bar** at the top of the window that shows the name of the program inside the window.

- A **menu bar** just below the title bar. Commands on that menu bar affect *only* the stuff within that window.

- A **toolbar** for quick access to commonly used menu commands.

- A **document area** where you do your actual work.

- A **status bar** with a hint line (at the lower left) and sometimes with indicators to keep you informed of settings that are relevant to that particular program.

Figure 5.2 showed examples of these features for WordPerfect, a program you may have on your computer.

Some programs, such as WordPerfect and others in the PerfectOffice suite, display the hint line on the title bar rather than the status bar.

Using a Program

The menu bar within a program's window is unique to that program. But there are common menu commands that apply to most programs, and you can start exploring these right away:

- To **create** a new document within this program, choose File ➤ New from the program's menu bar.

- To **get help** with the program you're using, choose Help from that program's menu bar. Generally, you can choose Help ➤ Contents to get to the Table of Contents or choose Help ➤ Search to get to the index for that program's online help. To exit help, click on the Close (X) button in the help window (*not* the program's window) as illustrated in Figure 5.3.

- To **save** whatever work you've accomplished within this program, choose File ➤ Save from the program's menu bar. Fill in the dialog box that appears.

- To **arrange** multiple documents within the program's window, choose Window ➤ Cascade from the program's menu bar.

- To **print** the document that's currently inside the program's window, choose File ➤ Print from the program's menu bar. Respond to any dialog boxes that appear.

To arrange multiple program windows on the desktop, right-click on the taskbar and choose an option from the pop-up menu that appears.

FIGURE 5.3

A help window for WordPerfect. To remove the help window, click on its Close (X) button.

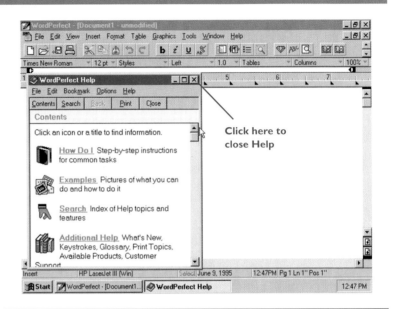

When you close a document or exit a program, you'll be given a chance to save any unsaved work. You should always choose Yes when asked about saving your work unless you're absolutely sure you *never* want to view, change, or print that document again in the future.

● To undo a recent action, choose Edit ➤ Undo from the program's menu bar.

● To close the document that's currently in the program's window, choose File ➤ Close from the program's menu bar. The document will be removed from the screen, but the program's window will still be available.

● To open an existing document that you've previously created and saved with this program, choose File ➤ Open from the program's menu bar. Select the name of the file that you want to open from the dialog box that appears.

● To exit the program, choose File ➤ Exit or click on the Close (X) button in the upper-right corner of the program's window. Both the document and the program will be removed from the screen.

Remember that you can try these techniques with just about any program that you start on your PC. Chapter 6 will give you some specific examples of these common features and at the same time teach you the basics of using your computer to write and draw on your PC.

Creating Shortcuts to Frequently Used Programs

Sometimes it's handy to be able to work with a file, folder, printer, or other object from *anywhere* you want—not just from its original location. To do that, you create a *shortcut* to the original object and then use the shortcut icon as you would any other. Shortcuts behave just like the original objects they came from. You can put shortcuts on the desktop or in any folder.

Keep in mind that shortcuts are just *links* or pointers to an object. They aren't the object itself and they don't occupy much space on the disk. If you delete a shortcut, the original object will remain on disk, safe and sound.

To find out if an object is a shortcut, just look carefully at its icon. Shortcut icons look like normal icons *except* they have a little shortcut arrow in the lower-left corner. Often their file names include the words "Shortcut to…."

Shortcut to Winword

There are several ways to create shortcuts, but the two methods described next probably will be handiest.

Like other icons, shortcuts have *properties*. To view or change these properties, right-click on the shortcut and choose Properties. Then click on the tab for whatever property you're interested in, make any necessary changes, and choose OK.

Creating a Shortcut for an Icon You Can See Now

To quickly create a shortcut for objects in the current window (or on the desktop), select the object or objects. Then either right-click and choose Create <u>S</u>hortcut or choose <u>F</u>ile ➤ Create Shortcut. A new shortcut, with the name *Shortcut to…*, will appear in the same place where the original icons are. You can then rename the shortcut, move it somewhere else, copy it, or delete it as you would any icon.

Using Drag and Drop to Create Shortcuts

Drag and drop is one of the most versatile features in Windows. In fact, you can use it almost any time you want to move or copy something from one place to another. The basic drag-and-drop steps are always the same; however, what happens when you drag and drop depends on what you drag and where you drop it. Here's how to use drag and drop to create a shortcut:

1 Find and select the objects you want to create a shortcut for.

2 Find the place where you want the shortcut to appear. For example, if you want to create a shortcut on the desktop, make sure you can see some empty space on the desktop. If you want to put a shortcut inside a folder, open the folder where you want the shortcut to appear.

3 Hold down the *secondary* (right) mouse button while dragging the selected object(s) to the place where you want to create the shortcut(s), then release the button.

4 Click on Create Shortcut(s) Here in the property sheet.

You may need to close or minimize some windows until you can see both the objects you want to create shortcuts for and the place where you want the shortcuts to appear.

Autostarting Favorite Programs

If you shut down your computer on a regular basis, you might want certain programs to reappear automatically when you restart your system. To do that, follow these steps:

1 Browse to, or Find, the icon that you want to autostart. You need to be able to see that icon on the screen.

2 Right-click on the Start button and choose Open.

3 Double-click on the Programs icon.

4 Now arrange the windows so that you can see the icon for the StartUp folder as well as the icon for the program that you want to autostart.

5 Now point to the icon for the program you want to autostart, hold down the *right* (secondary) mouse button, and drag the program's icon so that its ghost covers the StartUp folder's icon.

6 Release the mouse button and choose Create Shortcut(s) Here from the pop-up menu.

Nothing will happen immediately. But next time you restart Windows from scratch, the program you dragged to the StartUp folder will start automatically.

For more information on autostarting programs, search the Windows 95 Help index for *StartUp Folder*.

A Trick Way to Print Documents

Printing puts your document on paper. As with most things in Windows, there are several ways to print. The most common method is to choose File ➤ Print from a program's menu bar to print whatever document is currently displayed in that program's window.

But you can also print directly from the desktop:

1 Find and select the document(s) you want to print.

2 Then do one of the following:

● Either right-click on the document(s) and choose Print or choose File ➤ Print from the menu bar.

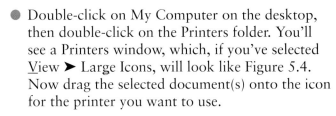

You can drag a printer's icon to the desktop to make a shortcut to that printer. Then you can print any document by dragging its icon from a folder window to the printer icon on the desktop!

● Double-click on My Computer on the desktop, then double-click on the Printers folder. You'll see a Printers window, which, if you've selected <u>V</u>iew ➤ Large Icons, will look like Figure 5.4. Now drag the selected document(s) onto the icon for the printer you want to use.

3 If asked whether it's OK to print multiple files at once, click on <u>Y</u>es if it's OK or <u>N</u>o to change your mind about printing.

FIGURE 5.4

The Printers window open on the desktop

For more details on troubleshooting printer problems, choose Start ➤ <u>H</u>elp, click on the Contents tab, double-click on Troubleshooting, and then double-click on *If you have trouble printing.*

You'll see some messages on the screen and a printer icon at the right edge of the taskbar. After a short delay, your document(s) will be printed. Printing usually goes smoothly, but if it doesn't, a Print Manager message will give you some tips about what to do next.

Managing Print Jobs

When Windows prints documents, it places them in a list called a print *queue*. When it's ready to print a document, it plucks the next document from the queue and sends it to whichever printer you specified or to the *default printer*. You can *manage* this queue if you want, and you can tell Windows which printer to use by default.

To get started with managing your printer, double-click on My Computer on the desktop, then double-click on the Printers folder. Alternatively, if the printer icon is visible in the taskbar, just double-click on that icon. You'll see the Printers window shown back in Figure 5.4.

A quick way to work with a printer is to right-click on its icon. After doing that, you can:

- Choose Set As De*f*ault to make this the default printer.

- Choose P*a*use Printing to pause all printing on this printer temporarily. When you're ready to resume printing, right-click and choose P*a*use Printing again.

- Choose P*u*rge Print Jobs to discard all the items waiting to be printed on this printer.

- If you're on a local-area network and want others to be able to use the printer that's connected to your PC, choose S*h*aring (see Chapter 12).

- Choose P*r*operties to set various properties for this printer. (You probably won't need to use this option; but if you decide to change the printer properties, have your printer manual handy.)

If you want to pause or delete specific items from the queue, you'll need to open the printer queue itself by double-clicking on the icon for the printer you're interested in.

A *default* is whatever you get when you don't make a specific choice. For example, when you right-click on a document icon and choose Print, Windows automatically picks the default printer (because you haven't explicitly told Windows which printer to use).

For quick access to your default printer, create a shortcut for it on your desktop.

If items are still waiting to be printed when you try to shut down Windows, you'll have a chance to decide whether to finish print-ing before shutting down or to cancel printing and shut down immediately.

Here's how to manage individual items in the queue:

- To pause printing for an item temporarily, click on the item in the list, then choose Document ➤ Pause Printing. Repeat this step when you want to resume printing for this document.

- To cancel printing for an item, click on the item in the list, then choose Document ➤ Cancel Printing.

How to Open a Document

Once you've created and saved a document, there are several ways you can reopen that document:

- Click on the Start button and choose Documents. If you see the name of the document you want to open, click on that name (or *Shortcut to <that name>*).

- Use the Find or Browse technique discussed in the previous chapter to locate the document's icon, then double-click on that icon.

If you have any problems opening a document, be sure to read the sections that follow.

- Start the program that you originally used to create the document and choose File ➤ Open from that program's menu bar. Choose the appropriate document from the dialog box that appears.

The document will open, already housed inside whatever program is *associated* with that type of document.

How Windows 95 Associates Programs and Documents

Occasionally, you might have some problems when you try to open a document directly from the desktop. Windows 95 might report that it doesn't "know" which program to open the document in, or it might open the document in some program other than the one you intended. Either situation is easily remedied once you understand how Windows 95 forges associations between programs and documents.

It's all done through the *Registry* and the three-letter extensions that get stuck onto the end of file names. For example, suppose you use Microsoft Word to type up a letter and then save that letter with the file name MyLetter. Behind the scenes, Microsoft Word automatically adds the extension .doc to the name you provide. So even though you only see MyLetter on your screen, the actual file name is MyLetter.doc.

The Registry keeps track of which document file extensions go with which programs. For example, the Registry "knows" that Word documents have the extension .doc. So any time you double-click on an icon for a document that has .doc as its file-name extension, Windows 95 automatically starts Microsoft Word, then loads the requested document into that program.

Hiding and Displaying File-Name Extensions

Normally when you're browsing around through icons and such, you won't see the extension that's tacked onto a file name. Instead, the icon for the document shows you the icon for the associated program.

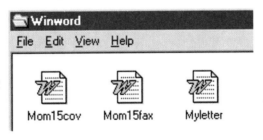

For example, the icon for MyLetter shown here shows the *W* icon for Microsoft Word even though there is no visible .doc extension on the file name.

If you do want to see the file-name extension, you would just follow these steps:

1 Choose <u>V</u>iew ➤ <u>O</u>ptions from the menu bar in the window that's showing you the document's icon and file name.

2 Choose the View tab, then clear (deselect) the option titled *Hide MS-DOS file <u>e</u>xtensions for file types that are registered.*

3 Choose OK.

Hiding and Displaying Directory Names

Those of you with prior DOS/Windows experience may feel more comfortable with file-name extensions and path names displayed. For example, you might prefer that a folder window display c:\msoffice\winword rather than just winword. To do that, follow steps 1 and 2 under *Hiding and Displaying File-Name Extensions.* In step 2, choose *Display the full MS-DOS <u>p</u>ath in the title bar.*

The file-name extension will appear in all folder windows with

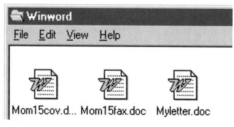

every file name that has an extension, as shown here (MyLetter.doc). In fact, that new setting will stick until you repeat steps 1 through 3 above and reselect (rather than clear) the *Hide MS-DOS file <u>e</u>xtensions for file types that are registered* option.

Creating and Changing Associations

If you want to create or change an association between a file-name extension and a program, follow these steps:

1 Double-click on the My Computer icon.

2 Choose <u>V</u>iew ➤ <u>O</u>ptions from My Computer's menu bar.

3 Click on the File Types tab to get to the dialog box shown in Figure 5.5. Then:

- If you want to change an existing association, select the type of file you want to change under *Registered file types* and then choose <u>E</u>dit. Specify the program that you want to associate this extension with.

- Or, if you want to create a new association between a file-name extension and a program, choose <u>N</u>ew Type and fill in the dialog box.

4 Choose OK to work your way back to the My Computer window.

If you need help while performing either of these sequences, just click on the Help (?) button in the highlighted title bar, then click on the option you want help with.

Your new setting will remain in effect for all future sessions. If you want to change the association again in the future, repeat steps 1 through 4 above.

If you need a quick reminder on how to do all of this in the future and don't want to look it up in this book, click on the Start button, choose <u>H</u>elp, and search the index for *associating, file types with programs*.

FIGURE 5.5

The File Types tab of the Options dialog box

This dialog box lets you create or change associations between documents and programs.

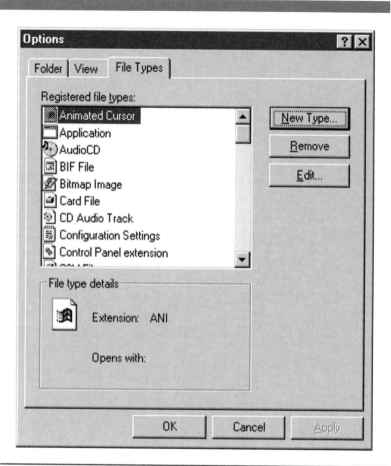

CHAPTER 6

Writing and Painting

Featuring

- Working with text in WordPad
- Working with graphics in Paint
- Things to know about any program

One of the best things about Windows is that once you've learned one or two programs, you've learned the basics of them all. In Chapter 5 we explained some of the basics already, such as how to start a program. We also reviewed tools that are common to most programs, such as the menu bar and toolbar.

In this chapter, you'll learn how to work with text and pictures, the two most common types of information on computers. To illustrate these techniques, we'll use two programs that come with Windows 95– WordPad (a word processor) and Paint (a drawing and painting program). What you learn here will work in many other Windows programs, including word processors, drawing programs, databases, spreadsheets, and more. At the end of this chapter, we'll give you some tips for learning *any* program quickly.

Working with Text in WordPad

WordPad is a mini word processor that lets you type text, format it nicely, and print it. It can store documents that Microsoft Word and several other word processors can use, and it can open documents created in Word, Windows Write, Notepad, and other word processors.

To start WordPad, choose Start ➤ Programs ➤ Accessories ➤ WordPad. If you like, you can begin typing your new text right away. Figure 6.1 shows WordPad with some text typed in and all the important parts of the window labeled.

The WordPad window with its tools visible

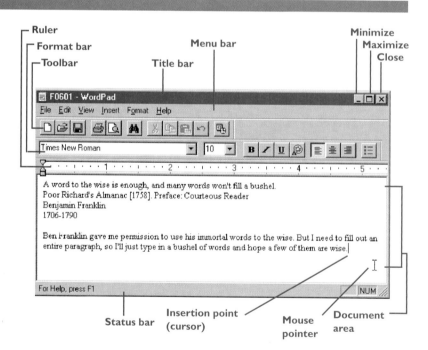

Ruler
Format bar
Toolbar
Menu bar
Title bar
Minimize
Maximize
Close
Status bar
Insertion point (cursor)
Mouse pointer
Document area

About WordPad's File Formats

WordPad initially creates files in Microsoft Word 6 format. These files have a .doc file extension and will run Word if you double-click on their file icons. To start with a different format, choose File ➤ New, click on either Rich Text Format (for formatted documents that launch WordPad when double-clicked on) or Text Only Document (for plain text documents that launch Notepad when double-clicked on), and then choose OK. Alternatively, you can use File ➤ Save As to save the new file in another format, as explained in Chapter 7.

Positioning the Insertion Point

The *insertion point* (or *cursor*) is the blinking vertical bar that indicates where the next character you type will appear or where text will be deleted if you press Delete or Backspace.

To position the insertion point using your mouse:

❶ Move the mouse pointer to wherever you want the insertion point to be placed in your document.

❷ Click the mouse button.

The insertion point will appear in the new spot. (If the mouse pointer is covering the insertion point, simply move the mouse slightly on the mouse pad.)

To position the insertion point with your keyboard, use any of the keystrokes listed in Table 6.1.

The techniques for positioning the insertion point, typing text, and selecting text also work in the text boxes of a dialog box.

Be careful not to drag the mouse while clicking, or you will select (highlight) text. If you select text accidentally, just press an arrow key (such as → or ←) to clear the highlighting and try steps 1 and 2 again.

TABLE 6.1

Positioning the Insertion Point with the Keyboard

To Move the Insertion Point Here...	Press This Key
Down one line	↓
Up one line	↑
Left one character	←
Right one character	→
Start of document	Ctrl+Home
End of document	Ctrl+End

When positioning the insertion point, remember these things:

● Always position the insertion point properly *before* you start typing or deleting text. If you forget to do this, your changes will appear in the wrong place! (Choose Edit ➤ Undo to undo a mistake quickly.)

● You cannot put the insertion point before the start of the document or after the last text you've typed in a document.

Is It an Insertion Point or a Mouse Pointer?

The mouse pointer and the insertion point are completely different animals that do different jobs and look different. The mouse pointer's job is to show where the mouse is pointed at the moment. By contrast, the insertion point indicates where changes will take place. Remember, just because the mouse pointer is positioned at a certain place doesn't mean that the insertion point also is at that same spot. When the mouse pointer is over text, it is shaped like an arrow or like the letter I (hence its nickname, *I beam*). The insertion point always appears as a blinking vertical bar.

● All that blank space below the last line of text in your document probably isn't text at all; it's just an empty part of the window. So don't be frustrated when you can't move the insertion point into that blank area. If you do need actual blank text in your document, position the insertion point and press ↵ as needed to add blank lines. However, it's usually a bad idea to insert a bunch of blank lines as a means of forcing text to start on a new page. Instead, just let the program break the text into pages naturally. Most word processors (but alas, not WordPad or Notepad) have features that let you control where pages break.

Typing Text

To type text, position the insertion point where you want the new text to appear and begin typing. What could be easier?

When you create a Word 6 document (the default) or a Rich Text document, WordPad automatically takes care of wrapping long lines back to the left margin when your typing reaches the right margin (this is called *word wrap*). For this reason, you shouldn't press the ↵ (Enter) key after typing each line in a paragraph. Instead, use ↵ only to:

● End a paragraph.

● End a short line of text or break one line of text into two shorter lines.

● Insert blank lines before or after a line of text. Each time you press ↵, the insertion point will move down to the next line and a blank line will appear. (If you press ↵ too many times, press Backspace as needed to remove the extra blank lines.)

Choose View ➤ Options to choose the default measurement units, word wrap, and toolbars for WordPad. Choose File ➤ Page Setup to set the paper size, paper source, page orientation, margins, and printer.

Word wrap is turned off for Text Only documents, which generally contain special system information that should not have any fancy formatting (including word wrap). When creating Text Only documents, you *will* need to press ↵ at the end of each line.

Fixing Mistakes

If you make a typing mistake, position the insertion point where you want to delete text (or select a chunk of text as explained in a moment). Then...

- Press the Delete (Del) key to delete the character at the insertion point or to delete selected text. (Repeat as needed.)

- Press the Backspace key to delete the character to the left of the insertion point or to delete selected text. (Repeat as needed.)

If you've made some other kind of error (such as deleting too much text or formatting something badly), choose Edit ➤ Undo or press Ctrl+Z to back out of the change.

Many programs, including WordPad and Paint, offer several levels of Undo, so you can choose Edit ➤ Undo (or press Ctrl+Z) repeatedly to back out of changes one by one.

Selecting Text

Often you'll want to change an entire chunk of existing text. For instance, you might want to boldface or underline a heading, change its typeface (font), or even delete it. To tell WordPad which chunk of text to work with, you must select (or highlight) that chunk.

To select text with your mouse:

1. Move the mouse pointer to where the selection should start.

2. Drag the mouse through the text you want to highlight. You can drag left, right, up, down, or diagonally. (In most programs, you also can double-click to select a word and triple-click to select a paragraph or sentence.)

You can combine mouse and keyboard methods. For instance, you can start by selecting text with your mouse and finish the selection with your keyboard.

To select text with the keyboard, position the insertion point where you want to start the selection, then use any of the techniques listed in Table 6.2. (Repeat the keystrokes as needed until you select as much text as you want.)

TABLE 6.2

To Select This Text…	Press This Key
From insertion point to line above	Shift+↑
From insertion point to line below	Shift+↓
Previous character	Shift+←
Next character	Shift+→
From insertion point to start of document	Shift+Ctrl+Home
From insertion point to end of document	Shift+Ctrl+End

Selecting Text with the Keyboard

If you begin typing when text is selected, you'll delete the selected text and replace it with whatever text you typed. Some- times this will be what you want, some- times it won't. If you replace text by acci- dent, choose Edit ➤ Undo to bring back the original text.

Figure 6.2 shows the WordPad window after we selected sev- eral lines of text. Notice that the mouse pointer is an arrow when it's resting on selected text.

To turn off (*deselect*) the selection and remove the highlight- ing, press any key listed in Table 6.1 (for example, press ←) or

FIGURE 6.2

The window after selecting text

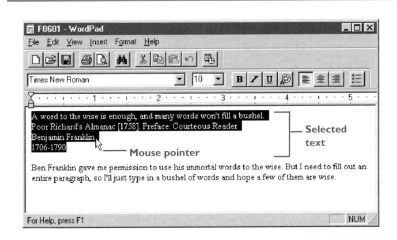

click the mouse anywhere in the document's text. Deselecting is handy if you decide not to change the chunk after all or your selection didn't highlight the right part or amount of text and you need to try again.

Changing Text

Changing text in your document is easy. If you know ahead of time how you want new text to look:

1 Position the insertion point where you want to make the change.

2 Choose menu options or toolbar shortcuts that apply the formatting you want (see Table 6.3).

3 Type the text that should have the new formatting.

4 Repeat steps 1 through 3 as needed.

If you didn't plan ahead and you want to change a chunk of existing text, do this instead:

1 Select the text you want to change.

2 Choose menu options or toolbar shortcuts (see Table 6.3) or press Delete or Backspace to delete the selected text. Or start typing to replace the selection with new text.

Some menu options and toolbar shortcuts are *toggles*. Choosing them once turns a feature on. Choosing them again turns the feature off. For example, you could select text and then click on the B button in the format bar to turn on boldface; do the same to turn off boldface.

TABLE 6.3

Changing Text in WordPad

To Choose This Text Appearance	Click on This Toolbar Button	Or Choose These Menu Options
Boldface	**B**	Format ➤ Font ➤ Font style ➤ Bold
Bullets	⦂☰	Format ➤ Bullet Style

TABLE 6.3

Changing Text in WordPad (continued)

To Choose This Text Appearance	Click on This Toolbar Button	Or Choose These Menu Options
Center align		Format ➤ Paragraph ➤ Alignment ➤ Center
Color		Format ➤ Font ➤ Color
Font name	Times New Roman	Format ➤ Font ➤ Font
Font name, style, size, effects, and color		Format ➤ Font
Italics		Format ➤ Font ➤ Font style ➤ Italic
Left align		Format ➤ Paragraph ➤ Alignment ➤ Left
Paragraph indentation and alignment		Format ➤ Paragraph
Right align		Format ➤ Paragraph ➤ Alignment ➤ Right
Size	12	Format ➤ Font ➤ Size
Strikeout		Format ➤ Font ➤ Strikeout
Underline	u	Format ➤ Font ➤ Underline

Figure 6.3 shows the screen after we made several formatting changes to the document from Figure 6.1.

FIGURE 6.3

The WordPad window after changing the text format

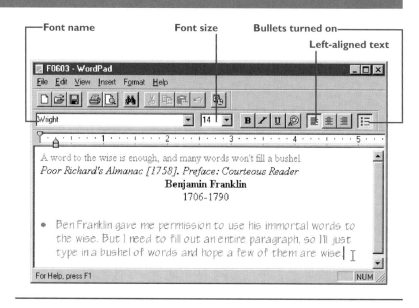

Font name   Font size   Bullets turned on
Left-aligned text

Setting Tabs

Some word processors offer several types of tab stops (typically left, right, center, and decimal). WordPad isn't so clever: only left tab stops are available.

Pressing the Tab key while you're typing text inserts a tab character (which looks like blank spaces) and moves the insertion point to the next tab stop. Tabs are used most often to format text into simple columnar lists (see Figure 6.4). Initially the tab stops are set every half inch, but you can change this if you want:

❶ To set tab stops for new text that you're about to type, position the insertion point at the start of a new blank line. To set (or change) tab stops for existing text, select the text that should have the new tab stops.

FIGURE 6.4

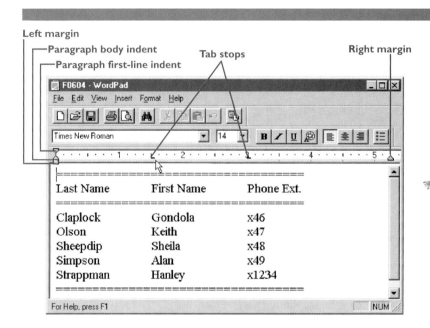

Left margin
Paragraph body indent
Paragraph first-line indent
Tab stops
Right margin

A document that's format-ted into columns with tabs

You can change the left and right margins and the indents for the first and subsequent lines of a paragraph by dragging the appropriate markers in the ruler.

2 Turn on the ruler if it isn't visible already (View ➤ Ruler).

3 Click in the ruler where you want the first tab stop. A tab-stop symbol will appear where you clicked. Repeat this step for each tab stop.

4 If necessary, adjust the tab stops as follows:

- To reposition a tab stop along the ruler, drag the tab-stop symbol to the left or right.

- To delete a tab stop, drag it down below the ruler.

Selected text will reformat instantly as you set or drag the tab stops in the ruler.

5 If you didn't select text in step 1 above, type the text (pressing Tab as needed).

Figure 6.4 illustrates a simple phone list that we formatted by pressing Tab once between each column on each line. Thus, to set up the phone-list heading, we typed **Last Name**, pressed Tab, typed **First Name**, pressed Tab, typed **Phone Ext.**, and pressed ↵. The double lines in the example are just a bunch of equal signs (=).

Here are some tips for working with tabs:

- Always use tabs, rather than spaces, to format text into columns. Even though spaces might look OK on the screen, you may get bad results when you change text in the columns or print the document.

- If you've ever set up tabs on a typewriter, you know that it sometimes takes a few tries to get it right. The same goes for setting tabs on computers. Be patient, and you'll master the art of tab setting in no time.

- Always put just *one* tab between columns. You may have problems later if you press Tab more than once between columns. If the text is too wide to fit without bumping against text in the next column, select all the lines that you're trying to format and adjust the tab stops or reduce the font size as needed.

Copying and Moving Text

Copying and moving text within a document is a lot like copying and moving objects on the Windows desktop, as discussed in Chapter 4.

You can copy or move text to a new place in the current document, to another document, or even to another program. There are two ways to copy or move—by using the Windows Clipboard or by using drag and drop.

Generally speaking, the Clipboard is best for when text is being copied or moved to another document or program or when the new text will be placed far from the original text.

Drag and drop is most convenient when the new text will be copied or moved just a small distance away.

Copying and Moving with the Clipboard

To copy or move text with the Clipboard:

1 Select the text to be copied or moved.

2 Place the selection on the Clipboard as follows:

- To *move* the selected text to the Clipboard, choose Edit ➤ Cut (or press Ctrl+X or click on the Cut button in the toolbar). The selected text will disappear from the document.

- To *copy* the selected text to the Clipboard, choose Edit ➤ Copy (or press Ctrl+C or click on the Copy button in the toolbar). The selected text will remain in the document.

3 Position the insertion point where the moved or copied text should appear. This can be the same document, another document in the same program, or a document in another program.

4 Choose Edit ➤ Paste (or press Ctrl+V or click on the Paste button in the toolbar). The text will appear in its new spot.

Copying and Moving with Drag and Drop

To copy or move text with drag and drop:

1 Select the text to be copied or moved.

2 Move the mouse pointer inside the selected text.

3 To *move* the text, drag it to a new place. To *copy* the text, hold down the Ctrl key while dragging the text to a new place.

When the mouse pointer is inside selected text, it will change to an arrow, as shown back in Figure 6.2.

The toolbox and color box are movable. Simply drag them to new places on the window.

Working with Graphics in Paint

You can use Paint to draw or change pictures. To start Paint, choose Start ➤ Programs ➤ Accessories ➤ Paint. Figure 6.5 shows a Paint window with all its tools visible.

The Paint window with its tools visible

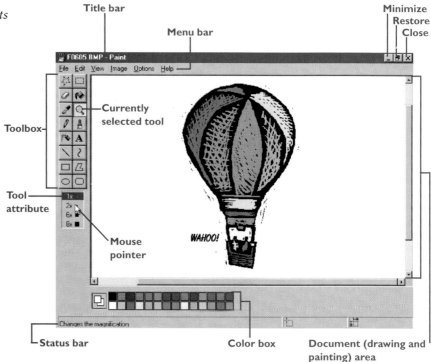

Title bar

Menu bar

Minimize
Restore
Close

Currently selected tool

Toolbox

Tool attribute

Mouse pointer

Status bar

Color box

Document (drawing and painting) area

The general steps for drawing with Paint are easy:

1 Choose a tool.

2 Choose any attributes that are available for that tool, such as magnification, opaque or transparent drawing, brush shape, or line thickness (if appropriate). Attributes will appear below the toolbox.

3 Choose a foreground and background color (as necessary).

4 Operate the tool by dragging or clicking in the document (drawing and painting) area.

Here's the quickest way to make a change in Paint:

1 Select the part of the picture you want to work with.

2 Right-click on the selection and choose options from the property menu or move, copy, or delete the selection.

Here are some other useful things to know about Paint before you get too involved in a project:

● To clear the image and start over, make sure no part of the picture is selected and then choose Image ➤ Clear Image.

● To undo a mistake, choose Edit ➤ Undo or press Ctrl+Z. Repeat as needed to back out of changes one by one.

● To view the picture without the clutter of menus, tools, colors, or the status bar, choose View ➤ View Bitmap or press Ctrl+F. To return to the normal view, click anywhere in the picture or press a key.

We'll explain how to choose tools and colors, select the picture, and do other jobs in a moment.

Choosing a Tool

To choose a tool, make sure the toolbox is visible (View ➤ Tool Box), then click on the tool you want to use. The tool button will appear pushed in.

Some tools have additional attributes that appear just below the toolbox when you click on the tool. To select an attribute, just click on it.

For example, the Magnifier tool (selected in Figure 6.5) lets you choose the amount of magnification you see the image at on screen (1x, 2x, 6x, or 8x).

Table 6.4 lists each Paint tool and briefly explains what it does and how to use it.

TABLE 6.4

Paint Tools and What They Do

Tool	Tool Name	What It Does	How to Work It
	Free-Form Select*	Selects an irregular shape using the chosen opaque or transparent background.	Drag around the shape.
	Select*	Selects a rectangular shape using the chosen opaque or transparent background.	Drag around the shape.
	Eraser*	Erases using the current background color and selected eraser shape.	Drag through the area to be erased.
	Fill with Color	Fills any enclosed area with the current foreground color.	Click in the area to be filled. If you click an unenclosed area, the paint will "leak" out.
	Pick Color	Picks up a color and makes it the current foreground or background color.	Click on an area to pick its color as the new foreground color. Right-click on an area to pick its color as the new background color.

TABLE 6.4

Paint Tools and What They Do (continued)

Tool	Tool Name	What It Does	How to Work It
🔍	Magnifier*	Magnifies the picture the selected amount. This is helpful for doing close work.	Click on the place to be magnified. To restore normal magnification, click on the Magnifier again, then click on the picture.
✏️	Pencil	Draws freeform.	Drag through the drawing area.
🖌️	Brush*	Draws freeform using the selected brush tip.	Drag through the drawing area.
🖌️	Airbrush*	Sprays foreground color using the selected spray size.	Drag through the drawing area.
A	Text*	Inserts text using the selected opaque or transparent background.	Drag a text frame to define where word wrap will occur. Choose options from the text toolbar (View ▶ Text Toolbar). Click in the frame and type the text. Move or resize the frame as needed. When done, click outside the frame.
╲	Line*	Draws a straight line with the selected line width.	Drag through the drawing area. For a horizontal, vertical, or diagonal line, press Shift while dragging.

TABLE 6.4

*Paint Tools and What
They Do (continued)*

Tool	Tool Name	What It Does	How to Work It
⌇	Curve*	Draws a curve with the selected line width.	Define a straight line as above. Then click on line where first arc should be and drag to form arc. If desired, click on line where second arc should be and drag to form arc.
▢	Rectangle*	Draws a rectangle with selected outline, foreground outline, and background fill; or background fill only.	Drag diagonally through the drawing area. For a square, press Shift while dragging.
◿	Polygon*	Draws a polygon with selected outline, foreground outline, and background fill; or background fill only.	Drag or press Shift while dragging through drawing area to define first line. Click or press Shift while clicking to define remaining sides until a closed polygon appears.
◯	Ellipse*	Draws an ellipse with selected outline, foreground outline, and background fill; or background fill only.	Drag diagonally through the drawing area. For a circle, press Shift while dragging.

TABLE 6.4

Paint Tools and What They Do (continued)

Tool	Tool Name	What It Does	How to Work It
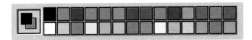	Rounded Rectangle*	Draws a rounded rectangle with selected outline, foreground outline, and background fill; or background fill only.	Drag diagonally through the drawing area. For a square with rounded corners, press Shift while dragging.

*Tool has additional attributes you can choose.

Choosing a Color

Most tools draw in color, using colors you've selected in the color box (<u>V</u>iew ➤ <u>C</u>olor Box).

- To choose the foreground color, *click* on a color in the color box.
- To choose a background color, *right-click* on a color in the color box.

The stacked squares at the left edge of the color box will reflect your current choices.

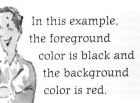

In this example, the foreground color is black and the background color is red.

Drawing or Painting

To draw or paint, follow these steps:

1. Select the tool, colors, and tool attribute you want.

Table 6.4 provides tips on using each Paint tool.

2 Move the mouse pointer to wherever you want to draw in the document area. The pointer will change from an arrow to a crosshair or some other shape.

3 Click the mouse or click and drag as appropriate for the selected tool. Repeat this step as needed.

If you want to draw an outlined and filled rectangle, for example, click on the Rectangle tool, then click on the middle tool attribute that appears below the toolbox. Click on the color you want for the outline, then right-click on the color for the fill. Now move the mouse pointer to the document area and drag diagonally until the rectangle is the right size.

Selecting a Picture

The first step in changing some part of a picture is to select the part to be changed.

1 Click on the Free-Form Select tool (the button with the dotted star) or Select tool (the button with the dotted rectangle) and then click on the Opaque or Transparent drawing attribute (see Figure 6.6).

2 Move the mouse pointer slightly outside the area to be selected.

3 Drag a frame or outline around the area until you've selected the area you want.

Notice that little *selection handles* appear at each corner and on the sides between each corner of the frame. (The next sections explain how to use these handles.)

If you need to turn off the selection (perhaps because you changed your mind or your original selection wasn't accurate), click in the document area outside the frame or click on the

FIGURE 6.6

The Opaque and Transparent attributes for a tool

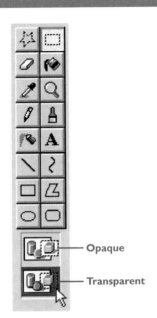

Opaque

Transparent

With opaque drawing, your selection will cover the existing picture if you paste or drag it. With transparent drawing, the existing picture will show through the selection.

Free-Form Select or Select tool again. The frame and selection handles will disappear.

Changing a Picture

To change part of a picture, select it as explained just above. Then...

- To delete the selection, press the Delete key. (The deleted area will be filled in with the currently selected background color.)

- To change the appearance of the selection, right-click and choose an option from the property sheet. You also can choose options from the Image menu.

For example, choose Invert Colors to reverse the colors (like a color negative).

Resizing a Paint picture can distort the image. Also be aware that Paint will use the current background color to fill in areas if you resize the picture smaller. If you don't like the results, choose Edit ➤ Undo immediately.

Stretching and Shrinking

Sometimes you'll want to stretch or shrink (resize) part of a picture. This is a lot like resizing a window:

1 Select the portion you want to resize (a frame and sizing handles will appear).

2 Move the mouse pointer to a sizing handle until the pointer changes to a *two-headed arrow*.

3 Drag the top handle up or down, drag the side handle left or right, or drag the corner handle in any direction (including diagonally).

The graphic will appear with its new size and shape.

Copying and Moving a Picture

Copying or moving part of a picture is similar to copying or moving text. To copy or move with the Clipboard:

1 Select the area to be copied or moved. (Be sure to specify whether the selection should be opaque or transparent.)

2 To *copy* the selection to the Clipboard, choose Edit ➤ Copy (Ctrl+C). To *move* the selection to the Clipboard, choose Edit ➤ Cut (Ctrl+X).

3 If you want to paste the image into another document or program, open that document or program and position the insertion point.

4 Choose Edit ➤ Paste (Ctrl+V). The moved or copied image will appear (in Paint, you'll find the image at the upper-left corner of the document area). If necessary, use drag and drop to reposition the image.

To copy or move an image with drag and drop:

1. Select the area to be copied or moved (if it's not selected already). Again, be sure to choose opaque or transparent selection.

2. Move the mouse pointer inside the dotted frame lines until it becomes a *four-headed arrow*.

3. To *move* the selection, drag it to a new spot. To *copy* it, hold down the Ctrl key while dragging.

Paint will use the current background color to fill in areas when you use drag and drop to move a selection.

Cheap Shots

We used a fancy screen-capture program named Collage Complete to take pictures of screens for this book. However, the Windows Clipboard lets you capture screens for free. To copy a screen image to the Clipboard, set up the screen the way you want it, then press the Print Screen key (to capture the entire screen) or the Alt+Print Screen key (to capture the active window only). Now paste the Clipboard contents into a document. For example, open the document that should contain the screen shot, click where the screen shot should appear, and choose Edit ➤ Paste.

Things to Know about Any Program

Believe it or not, you can learn most Windows programs very quickly. All it takes is a little experience (which you'll acquire over time) and the secrets we'll reveal in the next three sections.

If you skipped (or forgot all about) Chapter 5, go back there now for more of the basics of using programs.

Getting Started

To tour a new program quickly, start the program and then try these things:

- Study the program window carefully. Look for the menu bar, document area, and status bar. Also look for toolbars, toolboxes, rulers, and other doodads that will help you do jobs quickly. Figures 6.1 and 6.5 illustrated these items in WordPad and Paint.

- If a tool isn't visible, pull down the <u>V</u>iew menu and choose the option that turns on the tool. To hide a tool, just choose the appropriate <u>V</u>iew menu option again.

- If the status bar is hidden by the taskbar, try auto-hiding the taskbar so it disappears when you're not using it.

- Pull down each menu to see what the program can do. When a menu is open, point the mouse at an option and look at the status bar (or the title bar) for a brief description of what the option does.

- To find out what the buttons on the toolbar and other areas are for, move your mouse to the button and wait for a short description to appear near the mouse pointer.

- Most programs have plentiful online help. Look for help on the <u>H</u>elp menus and in dialog boxes that offer <u>H</u>elp or ? buttons.

- If an online tutorial is available on the <u>H</u>elp menu (or the program's start-up screen), by all means try it. Tutorials are a quick way to get your fingers wet and to learn the basic features of a program.

- In many programs, you can right-click on an area of the screen (or selected material) and then choose an option that's relevant to what you're doing now. Try this instead of hunting around for options on the menus.

To auto-hide, right-click an empty part of the taskbar, choose Properties, check the Always on <u>t</u>op and A<u>u</u>to hide options, and choose OK.

You also can press the universal Help key—F1—to get help anytime you need it.

Making Changes

Much of your work with a program will involve changing text or pictures. This is usually a simple process:

1 If you're using a drawing or painting program, select a tool.

2 Either tell the program where to put new material or select existing material to work with. (If you can't see what you want to work with, try using the scroll bars or a *find* command.)

3 Make the change. This can involve deleting something, changing its appearance, typing new text, drawing something, and so on.

If your latest changes did more harm than good, you can:

● Choose Edit ➤ Undo to back out of your most recent change or changes. (In programs that have several levels of Undo, you can repeat this step as needed to back out of changes one by one.)

● Or close your document *without saving* the most recent changes, then open the document again. Bailing out this way is best when Undo doesn't undo enough or isn't available.

Working with Documents

In Chapter 5 we reviewed some common menu options that all programs share. Now that you have some experience creating documents, let's look again at some options that can help you manage these documents. In most programs, you'll find these options on the File menu:

File ➤ Close Closes the current document and lets you save any unsaved work.

Some very common shortcuts that will work in a lot of programs include Ctrl+N (for File ➤ New), Ctrl+O (for File ➤ Open), Ctrl+S (for File ➤ Save), and Ctrl+P (for File ➤ Print). To verify these for a particular program, click on File in that program's menu bar and check out the shortcut keys listed to the right of some options.

File ➤ New Clears the screen and opens a new document window. You may be prompted to save unsaved work or asked to choose a format for the new document.

File ➤ Open Opens an existing document that's stored in a file.

File ➤ Print Prints the document that's on your screen. Often you can select a printer and choose how much to print.

File ➤ Print Preview Lets you preview the document as it will appear when printed. The preview dialog box usually includes buttons for printing the document and canceling the preview.

File ➤ Save Saves the current document. If it's a new (unnamed) document, you'll be prompted for a file name. If it's an existing (named) document, no prompts will appear.

File ➤ Save As Lets you save the current document with a new name or a different file format.

See Importing and Exporting Documents in Chapter 7 for more about file formats.

In this chapter, you've learned the essentials of working with text and graphics in Windows, and you've picked up tricks the pros use to learn new programs quickly. The next chapter explains how to share information among many types of Windows programs, including word processors, painting programs, databases, spreadsheets, and more.

Sharing Information between Programs

Featuring

- Understanding OLE
- How to embed/link using cut and paste
- How to embed/link using Insert ➤ Object
- How to manage embedded/linked objects
- Importing and exporting documents

When you write something like a letter or memo, all you want is the text (written words). And sometimes when you draw, all you want is the picture. But there are many instances where you might want to combine text and pictures.

For example, Figure 7.1 shows part of a sample newsletter that contains text (written words) and pictures.

FIGURE 7.1

Part of a sample newsletter containing text and pictures: clip art (the beanie and glasses), word art (the main title), and a chart.

A document can contain more than just text and pictures. For example, electronic multimedia documents often contain text, pictures, video, animation, and sound!

Regardless of how you want to mix and match text and other objects, you'll probably use a technique called *Object Linking and Embedding* (OLE, pronounced *olay*, for short). This seemingly complicated name comes from the fact that pictures, charts, and so forth are all objects. And you can embed (or link) those objects into any document.

What Is Clip Art?

Clip art is predrawn art that you can use in your own documents–a must if you (like us) can't draw worth beans. You can buy clip art at most computer stores. Also, a great clip-art catalog is available from Image Club at (800)661-9410.

While we can't teach you everything there is to know about creating complex documents in this one chapter, we can show you the basic techniques you'll use to embed just about any object in any document.

Understanding OLE

OLE is all about taking stuff that you created in one program and sticking it into a document that you created in another program. Figure 7.2 shows a fairly simple example using programs you learned about in Chapter 6. The screen is displaying a WordPad document with a picture from Paint embedded in it.

Clients and Servers

When you use OLE, two (or more) programs are involved. One is called the *server program* (or server application), and the other is the *client program* (or client application). In a nutshell, the difference is this:

Server Program: The program that provides the picture, sound, or whatever object it is that you plan to embed or link.

Client Program: The program that contains the document that will receive whatever object the server program "serves up."

Perhaps more simply stated, the *server program* can give stuff to other programs, the *client program* can receive that stuff.

FIGURE 7.2

A sample WordPad document with an embedded picture from Paint

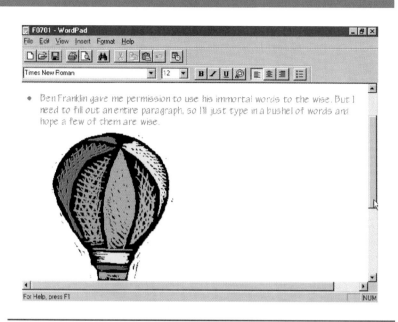

Linking vs. Embedding

Not all programs support OLE, and some require different steps than we've given here. If in doubt, check the documentation or online Help for the client and server programs. Look for the topics *OLE, linking, embedding,* or *object linking and embedding.*

As the name *object linking and embedding* implies, there are actually two different ways you can stick an object into a document. You can *embed a copy* of the object in your document, or you can create a *link* to the object. In a nutshell, the difference is as follows:

Embed: When you embed an object in a document, the document receives its own unique copy of that object. If you (or someone else) later changes that object, that change has no effect whatsoever on the copy in your document. Use embedding when you do *not* want the object in your document to change.

Link: When you link an object, your document does *not* receive its own copy of the object. Rather, your document just shows whatever the object happens to look like at the moment. For example, suppose you link a chart in your document, then close and save the document. Then you (or someone else) changes the chart. The next time you open your document, the chart you see will reflect the *current version* of that chart (rather than the chart as it appeared when you first put it in your document).

The only time you'd use linking, then, would be when you want your document to always show the up-to-the-minute latest version of an object. In most cases, you'll probably just want to embed a copy of the object as it looks, right now, in your document.

How to Embed/Link Using Cut and Paste

The cut-and-paste technique for embedding or linking an object uses the Windows Clipboard as a *holding area* for copying an object from its original server program into a document in the client program. You can use this technique to link or embed all or part of an object in your document. The general steps are as follows:

1 Open the server program (the one that can display the object or will let you create the object). Then create—or use File ➤ Open to open—the object to be linked or embedded.

2 If (and only if) you just now created the document *and* you want to link (rather than embed) that object, use File ➤ Save to save the object to disk. (If you are embedding or used File ➤ Open to bring an existing document onto the screen, you can skip this step.)

3 Select the part of the object to be linked or embedded.

4 Choose Edit ➤ Copy to copy the selected object into the Windows Clipboard.

Chapter 6 explains how to select text and pictures and how to copy and paste selected material.

5 Now open, or switch to, the client program (the one holding the document that will receive the object you just copied into the Clipboard).

6 In that client program, create the document—or choose File ➤ Open to open the document—that will receive the object.

If Paste Special isn't on the Edit menu or is dimmed, you cannot link or embed the object. However, you *can* paste a copy of it with Edit ➤ Paste. To change the copied object later, delete the object and repeat the copy procedure.

7 Move the insertion point wherever you want the incoming object to appear.

8 Choose Edit ➤ Paste Special to open the Paste Special dialog box.

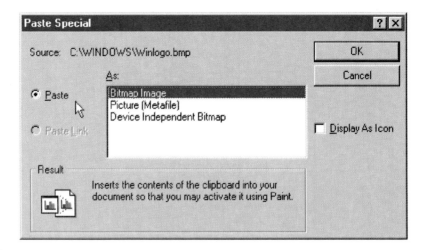

You can't tell by looking whether the object has been linked or embedded. Remember, the main difference is that a linked object will automatically be updated when you, or someone else, change the original object, whereas an embedded object will not be updated.

9 Click on the format you want in the As list or accept the suggested format (which usually is just fine).

10 If you want to embed the object, choose Paste. To link the object, choose Paste Link (if it's available).

11 Choose OK to finish the job.

The object will appear in the document. If a frame and sizing handles appear around the object or the object's colors appear reversed, just click anywhere outside the object to deselect it.

How to Embed/Link Using Insert ➤ Object

Here's another way to link or embed an object that's even easier than the first way. However, you can only use this technique when you want to link or embed an entire object (rather than just some portion of the object):

1 Open the client program and create or open the document that will receive the incoming object.

2 Choose Insert ➤ Object (or Insert ➤ New Object) to open the Insert Object dialog box.

3 Create a new object or link or embed an existing object as follows:

- To create a new embedded object from scratch, click on Create New (see Figure 7.3), then click on an object type in the Object Type list, and choose OK. The server program for the selected object type will open. Create the object normally. When you're done, do one of the following: If the program opened in a separate window, click on the Close button (X) (or choose File ➤ Exit and Return to…) and click on Yes if asked about saving your changes. Or, if the program opened in a frame, click outside the frame.

- To link or embed an object that's already stored in a file, click on Create from File (see Figure 7.4). Then type the object's file name (or use the Browse button to locate and fill in the file name). If you want to link the object, check the Link option by clicking on it; to embed the object, leave Link unchecked. Choose OK to finish.

The new object will appear in the document. Once again, if the object's colors are reversed or the object's frame has sizing handles, just click anywhere outside the object to deselect it.

As mentioned, different programs have different ways of linking and embedding objects. We can only give general steps here. If you have problems, search the client program's help screens or user's manual for *embed* or *link* to get more specific instructions.

FIGURE 7.3

The Insert Object dialog box when Create New is selected

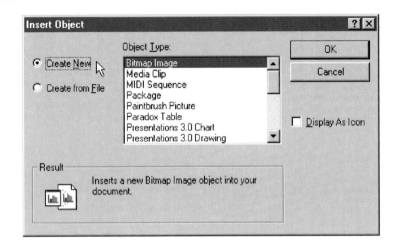

FIGURE 7.4

The Insert Object dialog box when Create from File is selected

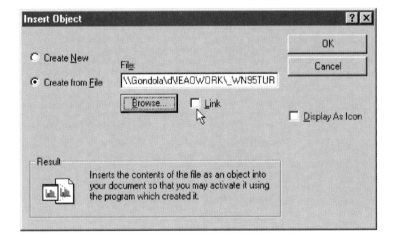

How to Manage Embedded/Linked Objects

Once you've linked or embedded an object in a document, there are many things you can do with it. First, however, you must *select* the object by clicking on it. Sizing handles and a frame will surround the object.

Once you've selected the object you want to work with, you can do any of these things with it:

- To resize the object, drag the sizing handles left, right, up, down, or diagonally (just like resizing a window).

- To move the object, move the mouse pointer inside the frame, then drag the object to a new spot.

- To edit the object, double-click on it, as discussed in the next section.

- To change properties of the object, right-click on the object and choose options from the pop-up menu that appears.

- To delete the object, press the Delete key.

Choose Edit ➤ Undo if you delete the object by accident!

Editing an Embedded/Linked Object

You can edit an embedded or linked object without leaving the client program. The quickest way is to double-click on the object. The object will appear either in a separate program window (as in Figure 7.5) or in a frame within the document (as in Figure 7.6). If it appears in a frame, the client program's menus and toolbars will be replaced temporarily by the server's.

Change the object as you would if you had opened the object in the server program. When you're finished, exit as follows:

- If the object is in a separate program window, choose <u>F</u>ile ➤ E<u>x</u>it and Return…, or click on the Close button (X). If asked about updating, choose <u>Y</u>es.

- If the object is framed within the client's program window, click outside the frame. The client's menus and other tools will reappear.

FIGURE 7.5

A linked or embedded object opened in a separate program window

In this figure and the next, we're using Microsoft Word and TextArt 2.0.

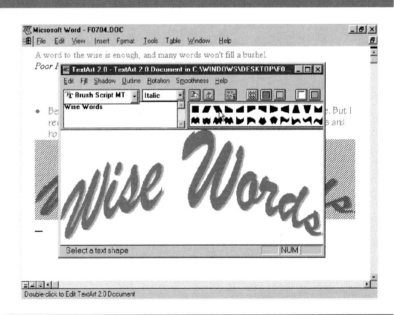

FIGURE 7.6

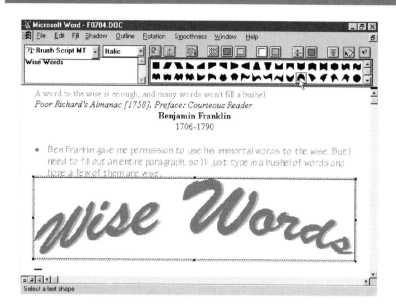

A linked or embedded object opened within the client program's window: the server's menus and tools temporarily replace the client's.

Text Art and Fonts

Text-art programs allow you to shape—and apply special effects to—text. The text-art program shown in Figures 7.5 and 7.6 comes with WordPerfect for Windows. Microsoft Office comes with a similar program named WordArt. If you don't have Office or WordPerfect, you can buy an independent text-art program at most computer stores or from the Image Club catalog mentioned in *What Is Clip Art?* earlier in this chapter. That catalog also offers a wide variety of fonts (print styles) that you can use in any Windows program—even if you don't have a text-art program.

Each type of embedded object has its own pop-up menu that appears when you right-click on the object. For example, the pop-up menu for a sound is different from the pop-up menu for a picture. But in general, the Open or Edit command on that menu lets you edit the object. The Play command on that menu (if any) just activates the object. For example, if the embedded object is a sound, the Play command will play the sound.

As humans, we tend to give all printed information *meaning* as soon as we look at that information. It's important to keep in mind that the computer knows *nothing* of meaning. All it *ever sees* are meaningless letters and numbers. The big trick to importing and exporting data is to *arrange* the incoming or outgoing information into a format that the other program can manage.

Here's another way to open an object for editing.

1 Right-click on the object.

2 If there's an ...Object option on the property sheet, choose that option. Then choose an Edit or Open option from the property sheet.

The object will open for editing. Now you can change and close the object as explained earlier.

OLE Can Be Complicated

Again, we need to emphasize that there are no universal standards that describe how *all* programs support and use OLE. You'll probably be able to wing it through most situations using the general techniques described here. But if you have problems, you may need to refer to the help screens or user's manuals for the client program, server program, or both.

Importing and Exporting Documents

Sometimes you're not so interested in sticking a picture (or whatever) in a document. Rather, you want to use a new or favorite program to edit a document that you (or someone else) created using *their* favorite program (which isn't the same as yours).

In some situations this is easy because both programs use similar formats for storing documents. For example, you could create a memo in WordPad, and then open and edit it using Microsoft Word without a hitch.

But life is not always so easy. Sometimes the two programs will use vastly different techniques for storing documents. And then the only way to get documents from one program to another is to *import* a document from—or *export* a document to—the other program's format.

How to Import a Document

To import (open) a file that's in another format, try this technique:

1 Start the program you want to import *to* and choose File ➤ Open.

2 In the Open dialog box, click on the button next to Files of type (or List Files of Type) and then click on the file type of the file you want to import. Figure 7.7 shows an Open dialog box with the Files of type list visible. After you choose a file type, the list of file names will reflect the selected file type.

3 Use the browse technique to locate the file you want to import.

4 Click on the file name you want to import and choose Open (or OK) or double-click on the file name.

If the program you're using can't import the type of file you're trying to open, perhaps the other program can *export* to an appropriate file type. The next two sections will go into more detail about exporting.

If the program that's doing the importing needs more information, you'll have to complete some more dialog boxes. But once you're done, the imported file will be visible and ready for editing, printing, or whatever.

Exporting to Another Program Format

Exporting to another format is just as easy, as the steps below reveal:

1 Open the file in the program you'll be exporting *from* and choose File ➤ Save As. If you're creating a new document, you can choose either File ➤ Save or File ➤ Save As. It's all the same.

FIGURE 7.7

An Open dialog box with the Files of type list visible

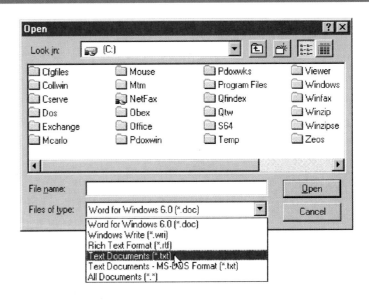

Never overwrite your original (unconverted) file with the exported (converted) version. If the exported file doesn't import smoothly, you'll want to have your original file available so you can try another export format later. Overwriting the original file will make retries impossible.

2 In the File name text box, type a name for the new file. For best results, *omit* the file extension.

3 Click on the button next to Save as type (or Save File as Type) and click on the file type you want (see Figure 7.8). Be sure to choose a file type that the other program can import.

4 Use the browse techniques from Chapter 4 to choose a drive and folder location for the new file.

5 Choose Save (or OK) to save the file in the new format. If the file exists already, you'll be asked if you want to replace the existing file. Choose Yes only if you're sure you want to replace the file; otherwise, choose No and return to step 2.

Now you can fire up the program that you actually want to use for editing the exported data. Use that program's File ➤ Open commands to open the exported document as though it

FIGURE 7.8

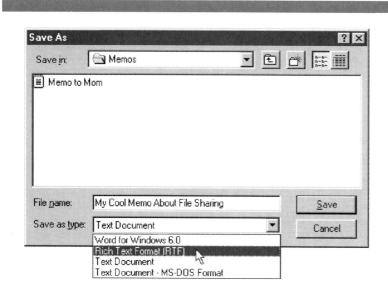

*A Save As dialog box with
the Save as Type list visible*

were just another document that you had originally created
with *this* program (the exported document will already be in
the format that this program expects).

Finding Common Ground

Sometimes two programs won't have import or export options
that match up. For example, suppose you've created a budget
in WordPad and now want to use it as an Excel spreadsheet.
As luck would have it, Excel cannot import WordPad (.doc)
files directly, nor can WordPad export Excel (.xls) files.

However, Excel *can* import plain text (.txt) files, and WordPad
can export those same files. So the solution is to pick a common format that one program can export and the other can
import. In this case, you could *export* your WordPad document to plain text format, then switch to Excel and import the
plain text document.

Most spreadsheets and databases
can import/export files in
the *ASCII Delimited Text*
format. Most graphics
programs can import
pictures in the
Windows bitmap
(.bmp) format. For
word-processing doc-
uments, try *ANSI text*
or *ASCII text* as a com-
mon format.

Importing and Exporting via the Clipboard

Sometimes copying and pasting with the Clipboard is the quickest way to import or export information. This is especially true if both programs expect the same basic type of document (for example, both expect text or both expect graphics).

For example, the Clipboard might prove handy for copying a paragraph from WordPad into a WordPerfect for Windows document on the same computer. Just follow the standard cut-and-paste routine. In this example, you'd select the text in WordPad and choose Edit ➤ Copy. Next, you'd start Word-Perfect and open the WordPerfect document, position the insertion point where the paragraph should appear, and then choose Edit ➤ Paste. Piece of cake!

And in a pinch, you can search the program's help file or user's guide for the appropriate buzzwords: *OLE, embed, link, import,* and *export.*

While we can't give you exact instructions for copying stuff between every program in the world, the general techniques described here will work in most situations. The important thing to know is that it *can* be done. In the next chapter we'll introduce you to a whole bunch of handy little programs that came with your Windows 95 program.

CHAPTER 8

Accessories Galore

Featuring

- Starting and exiting an accessory
- Tips for using applets
- Calculator
- Character Map
- Games
- Multimedia
- Paint
- Phone Dialer
- WordPad

Windows 95 comes with many handy little programs, all grouped under the general heading of *Accessories*, that will make your time at the computer more fun and productive. These freebie programs are often called *applets* because they are small, specialized applications (programs).

Windows 95 applets include several games; a word processor; a painting program; various system-management tools; and more. In this chapter we'll introduce you to the applets, show you how to run them, and offer tips for using the applets productively.

Starting and Exiting an Accessory

If you upgraded to Windows 95, your old accessories will appear on the Start ➤ Programs menus. Feel free to use them along with the new ones in Windows 95!

Starting an applet is easy:

1 Choose Start ➤ Programs ➤ Accessories. Figure 8.1 shows an example of what you'll see. (Don't worry if your menus don't exactly match the ones shown in the figure.)

2 Click on the name of the applet you want to start or, if the applet is on the Fax, Games, Multimedia, or System Tools submenu, point to that option and then click on the applet you want to use.

3 Use the applet according to its purpose. For example, play a game, complete a series of dialog boxes, or create and save a document.

FIGURE 8.1

The desktop after choosing Start ➤ Programs ➤ Accessories

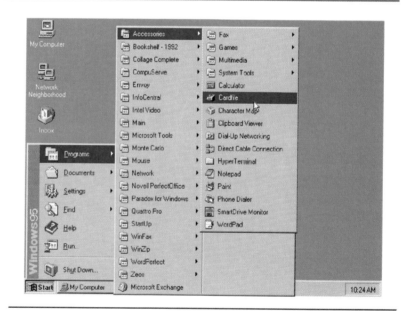

Figure 8.1 shows a fully loaded Accessories menu. If you did a Typical install, some accessories might not be installed. See Chapter 10 for help with installing new programs.

4 When you're finished with the applet, remember to close it. As with any program, you can use any of these methods to close an applet:

- Click on the applet window's Close button (X).

- Choose File ➤ Exit from the menu bar.

- In some applets, you can exit by clicking on OK right in the applet's window, or you can click on Cancel if you want to exit without saving any changes you made within the applet.

Tips for Using Applets

Most applets are easy to learn and use, mainly because they don't try to do a million things. Here are some tips to help you master the applets quickly:

- If the applet includes Help menus or a Help button, use them. They'll guide you through almost any task.

- If the applet dialog box includes a ? button, click on it, then click on an item in the dialog box to learn more about what that item is for. In many dialog boxes you also can right-click on an item and then click on What's This? to learn more.

- If the applet includes a View pulldown menu, put a check mark next to each option on that menu. Typically the View menu lets you turn on the toolbar (or toolbox), ruler, status bar, and other tools that will help you get the most out of the applet.

- If the applet includes pulldown menus, click on a menu, then slide the mouse pointer along the menu while watching the status bar. Repeat this for each menu to get a quick idea of what the program can do.

Most options on the View menu are *toggles* that can be checked (turned on) or unchecked (turned off). To turn the check mark on or off, simply open the View menu and select the appropriate option. For example, choosing View ➤ Toolbar will check or uncheck the Toolbar option on the View menu. When Toolbar is checked, a toolbar appears in the window; when it's unchecked, no toolbar appears.

For more
information
on shortcuts,
see *Creating
Shortcuts to
Frequently Used
Programs* in
Chapter 5.

● If the applet includes a toolbar, toolbox, or other buttons, move the mouse pointer to a button, then wait a moment for a brief description of that button to appear.

● To create a shortcut to any applet that you use frequently, go to the Windows folder in My Computer or the Explorer. Right-click on the icon/name of the applet and choose Create Shortcut. Then drag the new shortcut icon to the desktop.

● When in doubt, try it out! You can't hurt anything by using an applet. For most applets, experimenting is the best way to learn.

Next we'll take a quick look at some of the fun and handy accessories you'll find in Windows 95.

Calculator

Pop Quiz: What's $49.95 with 7.75% sales tax added on? To get the answer, choose Start ➤ Programs ➤ Accessories ➤ Calculator. Then click (or type) 49.95 * 1.0775 = to get your answer. (Round the answer to the nearest penny in your head.) Choose the Clear (C) button to start a new calculation or click on the Close button (X) when you're done.

Character Map

Your keyboard lets you type all the standard letters of the alphabet, punctuation marks, and numbers. But what about special symbols like © or foreign characters like ñ? You can usually find those kinds of characters in the Character Map.

Let's say you're typing in WordPad or Microsoft Word and suddenly need one of those characters. Click on the Start button and choose Programs ➤ Accessories ➤ Character Map. Click on any character to magnify it. If you can't find the character you want, try choosing a different font from the Font list.

When you do find the character you want, choose Select, then choose Copy. Close or minimize the Character Map and click in your document where you want that character to appear. Then choose Edit ➤ Paste or press Ctrl+V. The character will appear in your document.

If the wrong character appears in your document, select the character (by dragging the mouse pointer through it), then change the font of that selected text to whatever font you used in Character Map. In most word-processing programs, you choose Format ➤ Font to change the font of selected text.

Most sophisticated word processors, like WordPerfect and Word, have their own built-in special character sets. When using one of those programs, try choosing Insert ➤ Character or Insert ➤ Symbol rather than going through the Start button.

Games

To try out a game in Windows 95, click on Start and choose Programs ➤ Accessories ➤ Games. Then click on the name of the game you want to play.

FreeCell

FreeCell is similar to Solitaire. To learn how to play, choose
<u>Help</u> ➤ <u>Help</u> Topics from FreeCell's menu bar.

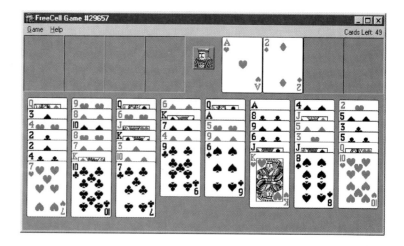

Hearts

Play the classic card game against the computer or connect to a
Hearts game being played on your network. Choose <u>Help</u> ➤
<u>Help</u> Topics from Hearts' menu bar for instructions.

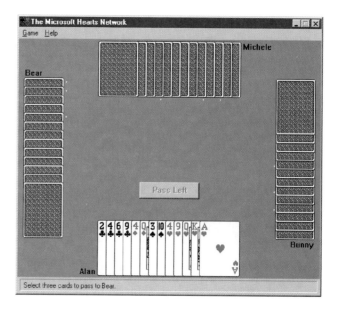

Multimedia

If your computer has a sound card and/or other multimedia accessories, you can use the applets in the multimedia folder to play around. Click on Start and choose Programs ➤ Accessories ➤ Multimedia.

CD Player

Play any CD you'd normally use in your stereo in the CD-ROM drive connected to your computer. Choose Help ➤ Help Topics from CD Player's menu bar for instructions.

Media Player

Play any audio, video, and animation files that are on your system or on the CD-ROM disk that's currently in your CD-ROM drive. Choose Device to select the type of medium you want to play. Choose Help ➤ Help Topics for more details.

Sound Recorder

If you have a sound card, use Sound Recorder to listen to sounds, add echo, reverse the sounds, and so forth. Choose Help ➤ Help Topics from Sound Recorder's menu bar for instructions.

If you have a microphone, you can also use Sound Recorder to record sounds.

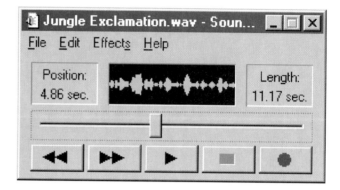

Volume Control

Control volume and balance on master and auxiliary sound sources, audio output, MIDI music, and compact discs.

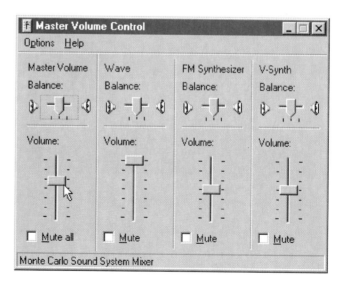

Paint

Use Paint (Start ➤ Programs ➤ Accessories ➤ Paint) to create pictures, or to open, view, print, and modify existing pictures stored in the Windows Bitmap (.bmp) format. See Chapter 6 in this book, and Paint's Help system, for more information.

If you need to convert other picture formats—such as Windows Metafiles (.wmf), Computer Graphics Metafiles (.cgm), and so forth—to or from Windows Bitmap (.bmp) format, consider purchasing a graphics-conversion program. We use *HiJaak Pro for Windows* from Inset Co. in Brookfield, CT; phone (203)740-2400, fax (203)775-5634.

Capturing the Screen with Paint

You can use Paint to print a copy of exactly what's on your screen at the moment (similar to the old DOS screen dump, for those of you who remember that). Paint need not be open to get started. Instead, just get whatever you want to print on your screen, then press PrintScreen (PrtSc) to capture the entire screen or press Alt+PrintScreen (Alt+PrtSc) to capture the active window only. Then start up Paint and choose Edit ➤ Paste from Paint's menu bar. You can modify the image to your liking and/or choose File ➤ Print from Paint's menu bar to print the image.

Phone Dialer

If you have a modem attached to your computer and to your telephone, you can use the Windows 95 Phone Dialer to *speed dial* any numbers you want. To get to Phone Dialer, choose Start ➤ Programs ➤ Accessories ➤ Phone Dialer.

If your modem is connected to your telephone and answering machine and you do *not* want the modem to answer the phone, you'll need to disable the modem's Auto Answer feature. See the manual that came with your modem for instructions.

To set up Phone Dialer for your personal use, choose Tools ➤ Connect Using and Tools ➤ Dialing Properties, and complete the dialog boxes. To add a number to a speed-dialer button, click on any blank button and fill in the dialog box that appears. For help with Phone Dialer, choose Help ➤ Help Topics from its menu bar.

WordPad

WordPad is a mini word processor that's built right into Windows 95 (see Figure 8.2). It's a great way to type a quick note, letter, or memo (though you wouldn't use it to create a lengthy report or book).

To start WordPad, click on the Start button and choose Programs ➤ Accessories ➤ WordPad. To learn some of the basics of using WordPad, see the section titled *Working with Text in WordPad* in Chapter 6 of this book.

FIGURE 8.2

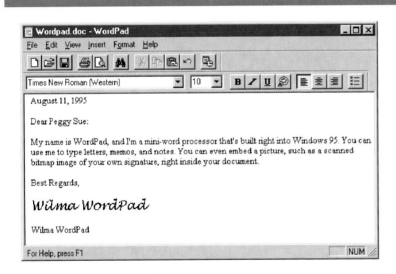

A WordPad document

In this chapter, we've introduced many of the freebie accessories that come with Windows. In Chapter 9, you'll learn some great tricks for personalizing Windows 95 to suit your own needs and work habits.

CHAPTER **9**

Personalizing Windows

Featuring

- Personalizing just about anything
- Customizing the screen
- Personalizing your mouse and keyboard
- Customizing the taskbar
- Personalizing your Start menu

You can personalize just about anything you see on your screen and the way you do just about anything. In this chapter, you'll learn how to personalize Windows to your own tastes and work habits. Keep in mind that everything discussed here is completely optional. So if Windows is behaving just as you like it, feel free to skip this chapter.

Just because you *can* customize Windows doesn't mean you *should*. If you're not sure what effect your changes will have, it's best not to change anything.

Personalizing Just About Anything

The appearance and behavior of Windows 95 and its objects are controlled by *properties*, which you can personalize to your own tastes. There are two main ways to change properties: either right-click on an object and choose Properties or use the Control Panel. We'll look at each method next.

Personalizing Things You Can See on the Desktop

If you can see an object on your desktop or within a window, you can probably personalize it. Here's how:

1 Right-click on the object and choose Properties from the property sheet. Figure 9.1 shows the Display Properties dialog box that appears if you right-click on an empty area on the desktop and choose Properties.

2 Click on the tab for the property you're interested in.

Chapter 3 explained how to get around in a dialog box. To learn more about an option in a Properties dialog box, right-click on the option and choose What's This or click on the ? button and then click on the option. Some Properties dialog boxes also have a Help menu that can take you to detailed online Help.

3 View and change the properties as needed. To apply changes you've made so far, click on the Apply button (optional).

4 When you're finished viewing or changing the properties, do one of the following to close the dialog box:

- To accept your changes, click on OK.
- To discard changes made since the last time you clicked on OK or Apply, click on Cancel.

The steps above work especially well with:

- An empty area of the desktop (see *Personalizing the Screen* below)
- The Recycle Bin icon

FIGURE 9.1

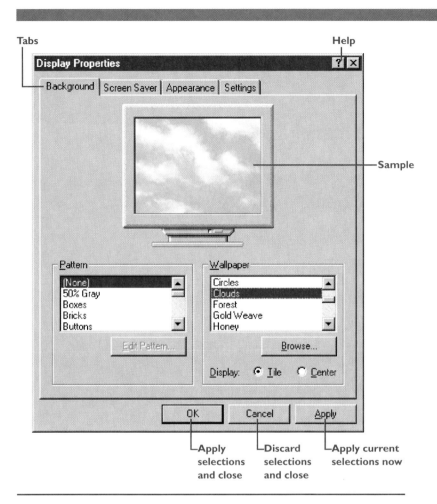

The Display Properties dialog box

- The current date and time (right-click on the current time in the status bar and choose Adjust Date/Time)

- An empty area of the taskbar (see *Customizing Your Taskbar* and *Personalizing Your Start Menu* below)

- Drive, folder, and file icons (see Chapter 4 for general information)

- Printer icons (see *A Trick Way to Print Documents* in Chapter 5 for general information on printers)

- My Computer icon (see *Using the Control Panel* below)

- Network Neighborhood icon (see Chapter 12 and *Using the Control Panel* below)

Using the Control Panel

Control Panel

The Control Panel also offers many ways to personalize Windows. To open the Control Panel, choose Start ➤ Settings ➤ Control Panel or double-click on My Computer on the desktop, then double-click on the Control Panel folder.

Figure 9.2 shows the Control Panel window and its many icons. Once the Control Panel window is open, simply double-click on an icon to open the related Properties dialog box or window. Then proceed as follows:

- If a Properties dialog box appears, follow steps 2 through 4 in the previous section.

- If you double-clicked on the Fonts or Printers folder, another window of icons will appear. To work with an icon, right-click on the icon and choose Properties, or click on the icon and choose the appropriate options in the File or View menus, or double-click on the icon to open it.

The icons in the Control Panel will vary depending on whether you installed optional components of Windows (see Chapter 10 and the Appendix).

Here's a summary (in alphabetical order) of the Control Panel options and what they do.

Accessibility Options Controls options for people with disabilities. These options let you adjust keyboard, sound, display, mouse, serial key devices, and other settings.

Add New Hardware Lets you inform Windows about new hardware on your computer (see Chapter 10).

FIGURE 9.2

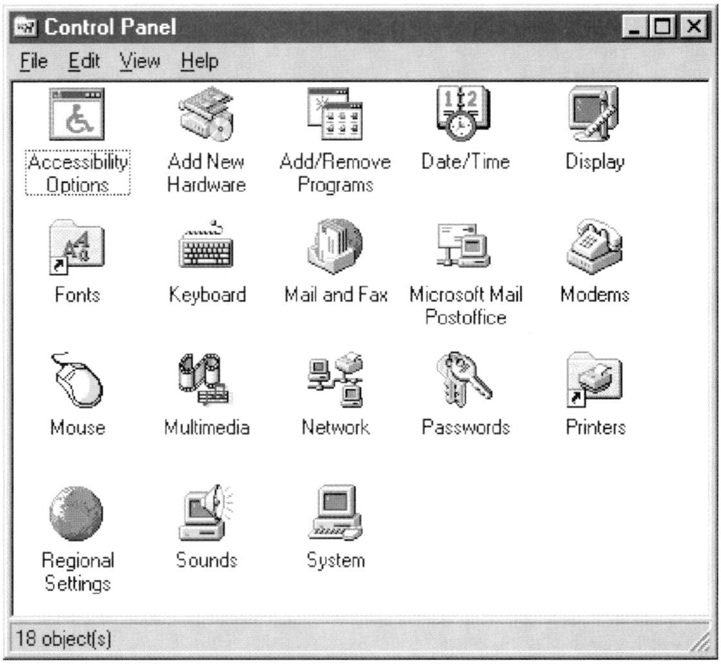

The Control Panel window and its icons

Add/Remove Programs Lets you add and remove programs and Windows components and create a start-up disk (see Chapter 10).

Date/Time Lets you set the date and time and select a time zone.

Display Lets you select desktop background, automatic screen savers, color schemes, color palette, desktop area, font size, and display type (see *Personalizing the Screen* below).

Fonts Lets you install and remove TrueType fonts and view and print sample fonts.

Windows 95 supports TrueType and Postscript Type 1 Fonts. Use the Fonts icon to install/remove TrueType Fonts. Use Adobe Type Manager (ATM) to install/remove Type 1 Fonts. Typically, when you buy a Type 1 font, you'll automatically receive a copy of ATM or some other program that can install those fonts for use with Windows.

For more about setting up a modem, see Chapter 10.

Keyboard Lets you specify keyboard speed, cursor blink rate, keyboard language and layout, and keyboard type.

Mail and Fax Lets you manage profiles for Microsoft Exchange, a program for exchanging electronic mail and fax messages.

Microsoft Mail Postoffice Lets you administer an existing Workgroup Postoffice or create a new one.

Modems Lets you inform Windows about a new modem on your computer.

Mouse Lets you control mouse settings including configuration of mouse buttons, double-click speed, appearance of mouse pointers, pointer speed, pointer trails, and mouse type.

Multimedia Lets you control settings for audio playback and recording, Window size for video clips MIDI output instrument, MIDI channel-assignment schemes, CD-ROM drive and headphone volume, and multimedia device properties.

Network Lets you manage network components, control file and printer sharing, identify your computer on the network, and determine how shared resources are accessed. (You can also get to this folder by right-clicking on the Network Neighborhood icon and choosing Properties.)

Passwords Lets you change passwords for Windows and other password-protected services, allow others to manage your files and printers from remote computers, and control whether other users of your PC can customize their preferences and desktop settings.

Printers Lets you add, remove, and share printers; control properties of each printer; and manage the print queues of each printer. (You can also get to this folder by double-clicking on My Computer, then double-clicking on the Printers folder.)

See Chapter 5 for more about printers.

Regional Settings Lets you choose which locale Windows uses for numbers, currency, time, date, and printer page size. You can then customize the number format, currency, time, and date for the selected locale.

Sounds Lets you associate a particular sound with each Windows event. For instance, you can have your computer play a sound of breaking glass when you exit Windows.

System Displays general information about your computer. Also lets you manage hardware devices, define alternative hardware configurations to be used when Windows starts up, and adjust file-system and virtual-memory performance.

For more about managing hardware devices, see Chapter 10.

Now that you know the essential steps for personalizing Windows, you should be able to explore most properties on your own. For the rest of this chapter, you'll learn how to customize the screen, keyboard, mouse, and the way you start programs (taskbar and Start menu).

Personalizing the Screen

It's easy to personalize the colors and other characteristics of your screen. You'll probably want to experiment with some different color schemes and other settings until you find the combination you like.

Opening the Display Properties Dialog Box

All your screen properties are controlled by a single dialog box. To get to that dialog box, use whichever method below is most convenient at the moment:

- Right-click on an empty area of the desktop and choose Properties, or

- Click on the Start button, choose Settings ➤ Control Panel, then double-click on the Display icon.

Display

The Display Properties dialog box (shown back in Figure 9.1) appears. The sections that follow show you how to use that dialog box to personalize your screen.

Personalizing the Screen Colors

To personalize your screen colors:

1 Click on the Appearance tab in the Display Properties dialog box.

2 Choose a color scheme from the drop-down list under Scheme. The sample windows above the list provide an example of how various windows will look with the color scheme you've selected.

3 To further customize the selected scheme, choose an item to color from the Item drop down list or click on that part of the sample. Then choose any of the available Size and/or Color options next to the selected item.

4 If the selected item contains text, you can also choose a Font, font Size, font Color, and Bold (B) or Italic (/).

5 Repeat steps 3 and 4 to color as many items as you wish.

Anytime a list is open or highlighted in the dialog box, you can press the ↑ and ↓ keys or the first letter of a description to cycle through sample items—schemes, fonts, colors—in the list. (If you find a predefined color scheme you like, skip steps 3–6 altogether.)

6 To keep your new color scheme for future use, choose Sa<u>v</u>e As and give your new color scheme its own name.

7 To apply your colors and return to the desktop, choose OK.

Figure 9.3 shows a really wild (if not outright nauseating) color scheme, with some custom fonts, that we've named Pink & Purple. (We're not recommending that *you* color your screen this way—it's just an example to show you just how wild you can get with this stuff!)

To return to the original color scheme, open the Display Properties dialog box, choose the Appearance tab, then choose Windows Default or some other setting from the <u>S</u>cheme drop-down list. Then choose OK.

FIGURE 9.3

A custom color screen with unique colors and fonts, named Pink & Purple

Personalizing the Desktop Background

The desktop background is the large area that all icons and windows cover. Normally, the background is just a solid color. But you can give it a pattern or even put a picture (called *wallpaper*) on the desktop background. Here's how:

1 Open the Display Properties dialog box and choose the Background tab.

- To texture the background, choose a texture from the Pattern drop-down list. If you also want to change the color of the background, click on the Appearance tab, choose Desktop from the Item pick list, and then choose a Color.

- Or, to put up wallpaper, choose an option from the Wallpaper drop-down list. (If you choose a small picture, you'll probably also want to choose Tile to fill the screen with that picture.)

2 Choose OK to return to the desktop.

When you're in the Background sheet of the Display Properties dialog box, you can also use the Browse button to pick any bitmap (.bmp) file to use as the wallpaper. For example, in Figure 9.4 we used a scanned photograph, saved as a bitmap image, as the wallpaper.

You can give the background a texture *or* wallpaper. But if you give it both, the wallpaper will cover the pattern.

Choosing How Much Fits on the Screen

Many modern display cards and monitors let you choose a *resolution* for displaying things on the screen. The general rule is, the *lower* the resolution, the *less* will fit on the screen (and the bigger each item will be). Figure 9.5 shows examples using exactly the same screen at three different resolutions.

FIGURE 9.4

*A scanned photograph
used as wallpaper*

Choosing a resolution is largely a matter of deciding which
one creates the least eyestrain for you. On a small screen (say,
less than 10 inches diagonally), you probably want to use a
low resolution, such as 640 by 480 pixels. On a medium-sized
screen, such as 10 to 14 inches diagonally, you might want to
use a medium resolution of 800 by 600 pixels. On a large
screen (15 inches or greater), you might find the high resolution of 1,024 by 768 to be OK.

A *pixel* is one tiny
little dot on the
screen. The more
pixels, the more
stuff will fit on the
screen.

Your best bet is to experiment to see what works for you. Note
that some settings you choose here may require you to restart
Windows. So, if you have any programs open on the desktop,
we suggest you close them and save your work before proceed-
ing. That said, to change the setting:

1 Open the Display Properties dialog box and click on
the Settings tab.

2 You might want to click on the Change Display Type
button just to make sure Windows knows what display

FIGURE 9.5

Icons and the calculator on screen at three different resolutions

Low resolution (640 x 480)

The higher the resolution, the more empty space is available on the screen—but at the expense of everything being smaller.

Medium resolution (800 x 600)

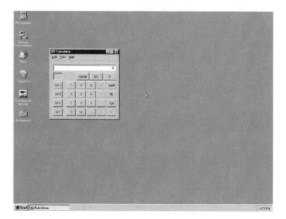

High resolution (1024 x 768)

adapter and monitor you're using. If you see something wrong, choose the correct setting and then close the dialog box with the X button. If the current settings look OK, click on the Cancel button.

3 If you wish, choose an option from the drop-down list. In general your choices will be 16 colors (fast, but only basic colors), 256 colors (better color, a little slower, and not supported by all monitors), or True Color (slow, but photographic-quality color). You may need to restart Windows after making a selection here. (If so, repeat steps 1 and 2, then proceed to step 4.)

4 Under Desktop Area, drag the little slider to the resolution you want (e.g., 640 × 480, 800 × 600, 1,024 × 768, or another available option).

5 Under some resolutions, you might also be able to choose a font size. This setting mainly affects text under icons. If you choose Small Fonts, that text will be very small. Choosing Large Fonts makes that text larger (and hence easier to read at high resolutions).

6 Choose OK and follow the instructions on the screen.

If you choose settings that your display card and monitor cannot handle, Windows 95 will restart in fail-safe mode. If that occurs, repeat steps 1 through 4 and choose settings that your display card and monitor *can* handle.

Choosing a Screen Saver

Computer monitors (and TV screens in general) are not designed to display a static image for long periods of time. If you leave an unchanging image on the screen for too long, you get what's called *burn-in*. That burn-in, in turn, makes the screen look fuzzier and out of focus.

To prevent burn-in, you can activate a screen saver. The screen saver is just a moving pattern (or blank screen) that kicks in whenever your computer has been inactive for several minutes. To activate a screen saver:

1 Open the Display Properties dialog box and click on the Screen Saver tab.

Whatever you do, *don't* forget your password, or you won't be able to get out of the screen saver yourself. There's no trick way to find out or change the password if you forget it. If in doubt, do not use the Password Protected feature!

2 Under Screen Saver, choose whatever saver suits your fancy.

3 If you wish, choose Settings to personalize the selected screen saver and choose Preview to see it in action. (After choosing Preview, you can just move the mouse a little to get back to the desktop.)

4 If you want to keep people from using your computer while you're away, you can choose Password Protected. Then choose Change and follow the instructions for defining your password.

5 Next to Wait, choose how long you want the screen to be inactive before the screen saver kicks in (three to five minutes is OK).

6 If your screen supports energy-saving features, you can change the settings for those features as well.

7 Choose OK to return to the desktop.

The screen saver will kick in *only* after the specified number of minutes (defined in step 5) passes with no mouse or keyboard activity whatsoever.

When the screen saver does kick in, any activity (even just moving the mouse a bit) will turn the screen saver off. But, if you password protected the screen saver, you'll need to enter your password before you're returned to the desktop.

Personalizing Your Mouse and Keyboard

If you have any problems using your mouse or keyboard, try customizing some of their settings:

The Microsoft Mouse and Microsoft Natural Keyboard offer additional custom settings. See the manuals that came with those items for instructions on installing and using the programs that let you change those settings.

- To customize the keyboard, click on Start, choose Settings ➤ Control Panel, then double-click on the Keyboard icon.

Keyboard

- To customize the mouse, click on Start, choose <u>S</u>ettings ➤ <u>C</u>ontrol Panel, then double-click on the Mouse icon.

Mouse

Each dialog box is self-explanatory, so you should be able to experiment with the options presented until you find settings that you like. When you're done, choose OK from the dialog box.

Personalizing Your Taskbar

The taskbar and Start button make it easy to start programs, get online Help, and switch between programs and windows. Initially the taskbar appears at the bottom edge of the screen, but you can drag it to any edge you want (see Chapter 3). You also can customize its behavior by following the steps below:

1 Right-click on an empty area of the taskbar and choose P<u>r</u>operties, or choose Start ➤ <u>S</u>ettings ➤ <u>T</u>askbar. You'll see the Taskbar Properties dialog box shown in Figure 9.6.

2 Select (check) or deselect (clear) the options described below to turn them on or off. The sample area below the Taskbar Options tab in the dialog box will reflect the options you've chosen.

Always on <u>t</u>op Select (check) to make sure the taskbar always appears on top of other windows. Deselect (clear) if you want to let the active window cover the taskbar. In general, it's best to select this option.

A<u>u</u>to hide Deselect (clear) if you want the taskbar to be visible at all times. Select (check) to reduce the taskbar to a thin line when you're not using it. To redisplay the hidden taskbar, simply point to the thin line with your mouse; to hide it again, move the

If you check Auto hide, be sure to check Always on <u>t</u>op also. Otherwise, you may have trouble finding the taskbar again. If the taskbar is nowhere to be found, press Ctrl+Esc, choose <u>S</u>ettings ➤ <u>T</u>askbar, then check Always on <u>t</u>op and click on OK.

FIGURE 9.6

The Taskbar Properties dialog box

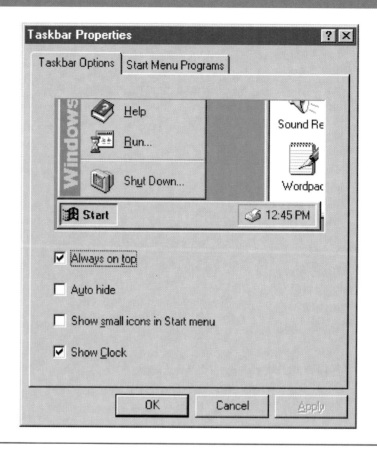

pointer off the taskbar and line. Checking Auto hide makes more space available on the screen and is especially handy when running programs in a maximized (or almost maximized) window. Figure 9.7 shows a Paint window with the taskbar hidden, while Figure 9.8 shows the same window with the taskbar visible. Notice how the taskbar covers the status information at the bottom of the Paint window in Figure 9.8, but not in Figure 9.7.

Show small icons in Start menu   Select (check) if you want icons on the Start menu to be small when you

FIGURE 9.7

A Paint window with the taskbar hidden

Status bar is visible

FIGURE 9.8

A Paint window with the taskbar visible

Status bar is covered by taskbar

click on the Start button on the taskbar. Deselect (clear) if you want large icons on the Start menu.

3 Click on OK to accept the changes and close the dialog box.

Personalizing Your Start Menu

The Windows 95 Start menu appears whenever you click the Start button in the taskbar. This menu lets you start programs, open recently used documents, and more. As you'll see, there are several ways to customize this menu.

Clearing the Start ➤ Documents Menu

Choosing Start ➤ Documents opens a menu of documents that you've used most recently. You can then just click on a document name to open that document.

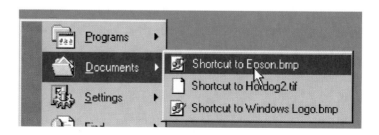

If the Start ➤ Documents menu becomes cluttered with old documents, you can clear it quickly with these easy steps:

1 Go to the Taskbar Properties dialog box (for example, choose Start ➤ Settings ➤ Taskbar). Then click on the Start Menu Programs tab (see Figure 9.9).

2 Click on the Clear button.

3 Click on OK to accept the changes and return to the desktop.

Clearing document names from the Start ➤ Documents menu has no effect on the saved documents. You can still get at them using Start ➤ Find, or My Computer, or Windows Explorer, or File ➤ Open in a program—whichever method is most convenient at the moment.

FIGURE 9.9

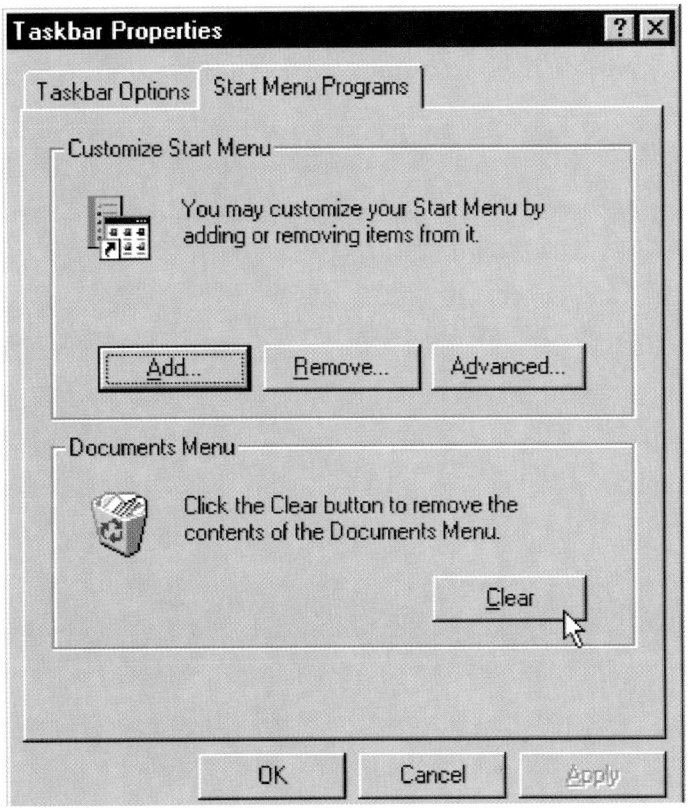

The Taskbar Properties dialog box after clicking on the Start Menu Programs tab

Adding Programs to the Start Menus

You can add your favorite programs to the Start menus and delete or reorganize those menus as needed. There are many ways to manage these menus, but we'll stick with the simplest methods here.

Follow these steps to add an item to the Start menus:

1 Go to the Taskbar Properties dialog box (Start ➤ Settings ➤ Taskbar) and click on the Start Menu Programs tab.

2 Click on Add to open the Create Shortcut dialog box.

3 Type the full name of the file to add as a menu item, or click on the Browse button, locate the program you want to add, and double-click on its name.

4 Click on Next to open the Select Program Group dialog box shown in Figure 9.10.

To quickly add a program to the Start menu, open the window that contains the program file to be added, then drag the program icon to the Start button on the taskbar. The next time you click on Start, that program name will appear near the top of the Start menu.

FIGURE 9.10

The Select Program Group dialog box lets you choose which menu will contain the new option.

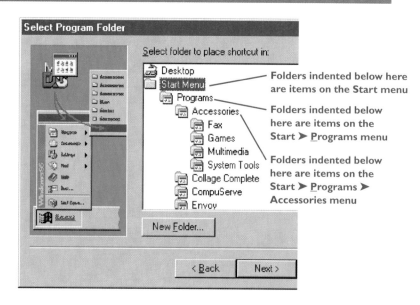

5 Click on the folder (menu) that should contain the new option. For example, click on Start Menu to put the option on the Start menu that appears when you click on the Start button in the taskbar, or click on Programs to put the option on the Start ➤ Programs menu. (If you need to create a new folder, click on the folder that should contain the new folder, then click on New Folder and type a name for the folder.)

6 Click on Next, then type the name you want to appear on the menu (or accept the suggested name).

7 If prompted, select an icon to use for the menu option.

8 Click on Finish to return to the Taskbar Properties dialog box (Figure 9.9). From here you can click on Add, Remove, or Advanced to customize the Start menu further, or click on OK to return to the desktop.

What Is the Start Menu, Really?

The Windows 95 Start menu is just a folder named Start Menu within the Windows folder in My Computer. What's inside Start Menu? Just more folders (including one named Programs) and a bunch of shortcuts to program files.

Windows treats the Start Menu folder and its subfolders specially, so you can run programs and customize the Start menus easily. As an alternative to the Start Menu Programs tools discussed here, you can use techniques from Chapter 4 to create folders and shortcuts, to delete objects, and to rearrange objects within these special folders. The results will be the same.

Deleting Programs from the Start Menus

Don't panic. Deleting items from the Start menus removes the shortcut links only; it has no effect on the actual program. You can still find and start the program using Start ➤ Find, or Windows Explorer, or My Computer, or Start ➤ Run—whichever method is most convenient.

Deleting options from the Start menus is just as easy as adding them. Here's one quick way to do it:

1 Go to the Taskbar Properties dialog box (choose Start ➤ Settings ➤ Taskbar) and click on the Start Menu Programs tab.

2 Click on Remove to open the Remove Shortcuts/Folders dialog box shown in Figure 9.11.

3 Double-click on folders or click on the plus signs (+) until you find the folder or program you want to delete. Now click on the object to be deleted and click on Remove. If you're prompted to confirm the deletion of a folder, click on Yes.

FIGURE 9.11

Use the Remove Shortcuts/Folders dialog box to delete options from the Start menus.

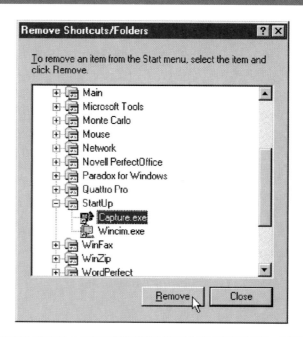

4 Repeat step 3 until you've deleted all the items you want, then click on Close to return to the Taskbar Properties dialog box. You can then click on <u>A</u>dd, <u>R</u>emove, or A<u>d</u>vanced to customize the Start menu further, or click on OK to return to the desktop.

Using Explorer to Manage the Start Menus

Windows Explorer (see Chapter 4) offers another way to add and remove items on the Start menus, and it is the quickest way to rearrange menu items. Here's how to manage your Start menus with Explorer:

1 Go to the Taskbar Properties dialog box (choose Start ➤ <u>S</u>ettings ➤ <u>T</u>askbar) and click on the Start Menu Programs tab.

2 Click on A<u>d</u>vanced to open the Exploring - Start Menu dialog box shown in Figure 9.12.

FIGURE 9.12

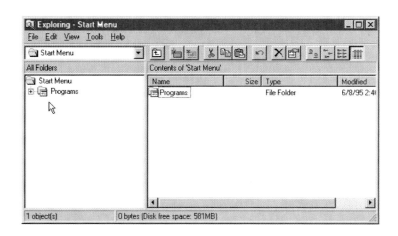

Use Windows Explorer to quickly add, delete, and rearrange items on the Start menus.

For more information about Explorer, see Chapter 4. Alternatively, choose Help ➤ Help Topics from the Exploring Window's menu bar, click on the Index tab, type **Windows Explorer**, and then double-click on the topic you want.

3 Use normal Windows Explorer techniques to set up your Start menus. Here are a few tips to get you started:

● To put items on the Start menu or its submenus, place them in the Start Menu folder or an appropriate folder below the Start Menu folder.

● To see the levels below a folder in the left side of the window, click on the plus sign (+) next to the folder. To hide the levels again, click on the minus sign (-) next to the folder.

● To open a folder, click on it in the left side of the window or double-click on it in the right side.

● To delete a folder or shortcut, click on the object, then press Delete and click on <u>Y</u>es.

● To create a new folder, open the folder that should contain the new folder. Then choose <u>F</u>ile ➤ <u>N</u>ew ➤ <u>F</u>older, type the new folder name, and press ↵.

● To create a new menu item (shortcut) in the currently selected folder, choose <u>F</u>ile ➤ <u>N</u>ew ➤ <u>S</u>hortcut and complete the dialog boxes that appear.

● To move object(s), make sure you can see the object(s) to be moved and the place where you want to move them. Then select the object(s) and right-drag the objects to their new location. Release the mouse button and click on <u>M</u>ove Here.

In this chapter, you learned how to personalize Windows to your own working style. Here we've covered in detail only those features that most people are likely to use. But you should feel free to experiment with any of the other icons listed under *Using the Control Panel* earlier in this chapter to further personalize Windows 95 to your own needs and tastes.

CHAPTER 10

Maintaining Your Computer

Featuring

- Installing new gadgets
- Installing new programs
- Tuning up for maximum performance
- Formatting a floppy disk
- Backing up your files
- Compressing disks

In this chapter, you'll learn the basics of maintaining your computer and safeguarding your programs and documents. Topics include how to tell Windows about updated hardware components, how to install programs and Windows system software, and how to maintain your disks and back up your files. Windows makes all these jobs easy, even for nontechnical folks!

The Appendix explains how to install Windows 95 from scratch. In this chapter, we'll focus on ways to install new gadgets *after* you've installed Windows 95 on your computer.

Installing New Gadgets

You may have heard some of these computer terms at one time or another: *hardware*, *devices*, *peripherals*. These are all just terms to describe gadgets that can be hooked to a computer. For example, printers, keyboards, mice, monitors, modems, CD-ROM drives, and sound systems are all *hardware*.

Before Windows 95, adding new hardware to your computer was something that most people couldn't do without professional help. But thanks to *plug and play* features in Windows 95, even novice users can plug in a new device, tell Windows about that device, and have everything work perfectly.

A True Story about Plug and Play

Elizabeth borrowed a computer from Alan while waiting for her new machine to arrive. Already installed on Alan's machine were Windows 3.11 (a predecessor to Windows 95) and a network and cable. Impatient to try the new machine, Elizabeth hooked the cable to a nearby computer on her Windows 3.11 network, then ran the Network Setup program, which asked a lot of technical questions she didn't know the answers to. After several futile tries to get the machines talking, she waved her white flag of surrender.

Knowing she'd be replacing Windows 3.11 with Windows 95 anyway, Elizabeth decided to gamble that Windows 95 could set up the network on its own. So, she fired up the Windows 95 setup program on Alan's computer, answered a few simple questions, and let 'er rip. In no time flat the network came up smooth as silk, and all the computers communicated perfectly!

Opening the Control Panel

The Control Panel offers the quickest route to installing new gadgets and programs. To open the Control Panel, use either of the methods below:

- Choose Start ➤ Settings ➤ Control Panel or
- Double-click on *My Computer* on the desktop, then double-click on the Control Panel folder.

Figure 10.1 shows a sample Control Panel window.

FIGURE 10.1

Use the Control Panel to inform Windows 95 about any new, changed, or deleted hardware on your computer.

Hooking Up the Hardware

Even a novice can connect cables for printers, modems, keyboards, and power without much trouble. In most cases, it's just a matter of matching square pegs to square holes and round pegs to round holes. But you should *always* read the manufacturer's instructions, just to play it safe. In most cases, it's especially important to shut down Windows and turn off *everything* before you go plugging things into the computer.

Some tasks require opening the computer's case and getting inside the machine. For example, internal network cards, modems, fax modems, display cards, and disk drives must be installed inside the computer's case. If you're skittish about playing around inside the guts of your system, consider hiring a professional to install these internal devices.

Adding a New Gadget

Installing new hardware typically involves these three general steps:

- Install the hardware according to the manufacturer's instructions. Run any test programs that come with the hardware to make sure everything is working correctly.

- Run the appropriate hardware-installation wizard to tell Windows about the new hardware. See *Running the Hardware Wizards*, below.

- Install any programs that come with the device, as per the manufacturer's instructions (or by following the techniques described under *Installing New Programs* later in this chapter).

If a test program expects you to start from a DOS prompt, choose Start ➤ Shutdown ➤ Restart the computer in MS-DOS mode? ➤ Yes. You'll be taken to a C prompt that behaves just like the DOS command prompt. After testing, you can restart Windows by typing **win** and pressing ↵, or by pressing Ctrl+Alt+Del.

Running the Hardware Wizards

To run a hardware-installation wizard:

1 Go to the Control Panel as explained earlier.

2 Double-click on the Add New Hardware icon to open the Hardware Installation Wizard dialog box.

Add New Hardware

3 Click on the Next button to continue to the screen shown in Figure 10.2.

4 Do one of the following to get the ball rolling:

● To detect all the installed hardware on your computer automatically, click on *Yes (Recommended)*, and then click on Next. This is handy if you've made many changes to your hardware or you aren't sure what's installed and what isn't.

● To tell Windows about a specific new hardware device, click on *No*, click on Next, and then click on the hardware type in the list that appears. Choose this option if you're in a hurry and know what kind of device you just hooked up.

Here are two shortcut alternatives to steps 1 through 4. To add a new printer, double-click on the Printers folder in the Control Panel or My Computer, then double-click on Add Printer. To install a modem, double-click on the Modems icon in the Control Panel. Now continue with step 5.

FIGURE 10.2

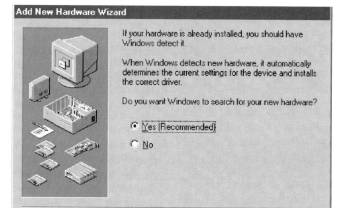

Use the Add New Hardware Wizard to let Windows detect installed hardware automatically or to install specific hardware.

Let Windows 95 do as much of the work as possible. For example, if asked whether you want the wizard to detect a device automatically, by all means let it do so.

If Windows is having a problem with an installed device, that device will be marked with a universal "NO" symbol (a circle with a slash) in the Device Manager list. Usually the quickest way to fix the problem is to delete the marked device from the list. Then return to the Hardware Installation Wizard and let the wizard detect and install the device properly.

5 Click on Next to continue the installation. The remaining steps depend on the option you chose in step 4, but you should have no trouble following the instructions. When you reach the last dialog box, click on Finish.

Windows will install the hardware and update settings as needed. If any conflicts exist between new and existing hardware, a Hardware Conflict Troubleshooter dialog box will help you correct the problem.

Using the Device Manager

You can use the Device Manager to review, print, and change settings for devices and to remove devices at any time. Be careful with this! In particular, you should not change or remove any device unless you know what you're doing. If your hardware has gone haywire, try using the troubleshooting techniques described below under *Solving Hardware Problems* or return to the Hardware Installation Wizard and let it detect all the installed hardware automatically.

To manage devices on your computer:

1 Open the Control Panel, double-click on the System icon, and then click on the Device Manager tab in the System Properties dialog box.

2 To view the devices by device type (the most useful arrangement), click on *View devices by type*. The System Properties dialog box will resemble Figure 10.3.

3 Pick a category or device as follows:

- To see the devices within a category, click on the plus sign (+) next to that category. (To hide the devices, click on the minus sign (-) next to a category.)

FIGURE 10.3

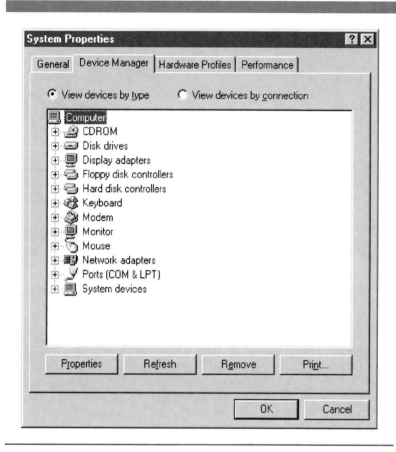

Use the Device Manager to review properties of a device, refresh the list of devices, remove a device, or print a summary of properties for devices.

To update the list of devices at any time, click on Refresh and wait a moment.

● To select a category, click on the category name.

● To select a device, click on the device name.

4 Use the buttons described below to view, remove, or print information about the selected device or category:

● To view or change properties for the selected device, click on Properties. Then click on the appropriate tabs in the Properties dialog box and make changes as needed. When you're finished, click on OK.

If you need to find an available IRQ to install a new device, here's a quick and easy way to do so. Double-click on Computer at the top of the device list. Then click on the Interrupt request (IRQ) option. Available (unused) IRQs do *not* show up on the list.

- To remove the selected device, click on R<u>e</u>move and read the warning carefully. If you're sure you want to remove the device, click on OK; otherwise, click on Cancel or press Esc.

- To print information about the selected category or device, or the system, click on Pri<u>n</u>t. Complete the Print dialog box and choose OK.

5 When you're finished using the Device Manager, click on Cancel.

Solving Hardware Problems

It's a sad fact of computer life that hardware problems happen. Sometimes hardware malfunctions for some unknown reason; sometimes it's just set up incorrectly. Fortunately, Windows 95 makes it pretty easy to get your hardware back on track. Here are some things you can do:

We've tried these troubleshooters to solve problems on our own computers, and they really work!

- Use one of the step-by-step troubleshooting topics in Help. To begin, choose Start ➤ <u>H</u>elp, click on the Contents tab, and double-click on Troubleshooting. Now double-click on the topic for whatever ails you (for example, *trouble with printing*, *dialing*, or *hardware conflicts*).

- Use the troubleshooting dialog boxes that pop up when Windows discovers a problem.

- Use the online Help to get general information about hardware. Choose Start ➤ <u>H</u>elp and click on the Index tab. Then type **hardware** and double-click on the appropriate topic.

Installing New Programs

Anything that's stored on a disk is generally referred to as *software*. Thus, all your programs and all the documents you create are software.

When you want to move or copy a document from one computer to another, you can just use My Computer or Explorer to copy the document from one computer's hard disk to a floppy. Then on the other computer, use My Computer or Explorer to copy the document from the floppy onto that computer's hard disk.

But copying programs is not always so simple. A new program typically has to be *installed* on a computer. The installation procedure does several things: It creates a folder (and perhaps subfolders) for the program, ensures that the program itself and any supporting files are copied, it tweaks the program to work best on your system, adds an icon to one of the Start menus, and so forth.

Installing a New Windows Program

Let's say you've just bought a new Windows word processor at your local Computorama and you're anxious to start working with it. You open the box only to find scads of floppy disks or a CD-ROM disk, tons of manuals, and a bunch of advertising and registration cards.

What do you do next? Well, you *should* read the installation instructions that come with the program. But if you're in a hurry (or the instructions don't seem to make any sense), try these easy steps instead:

1 Grab the floppy disks or CD-ROM for your new program. If you're installing from floppy disks, find one labeled something like *Setup Disk 1* or *Install Disk 1*.

It's rarely sufficient just to copy program files from floppy disks to a hard disk, because the program files are usually compressed. You need to go through the Setup or Install procedure to decompress and copy those files to your hard disk.

2 Open the Control Panel, double-click on the Add/Remove Programs icon, and then click on the Install/Uninstall tab to open the dialog box shown in Figure 10.4.

3 Click on the Install button to open the *Install program from floppy or CD-ROM* wizard.

FIGURE 10.4

The Install/Uninstall page of the Add/Remove Programs Properties dialog box makes it easy to add or remove programs.

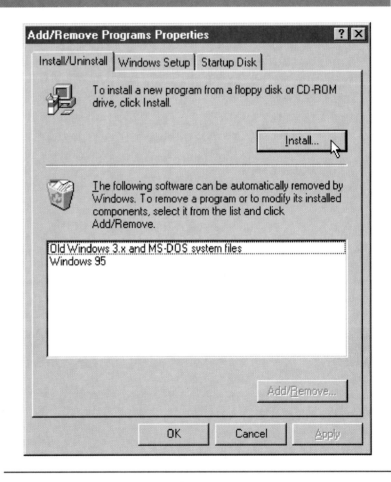

④ Insert the correct installation floppy or CD-ROM into the drive, click on the Next button, and follow the prompts that appear.

The installation floppy is almost always going to be Disk #1.

When the installation is complete, put the original floppy disks in a safe place. That way, if you or someone else ever accidentally erases the installed program from your hard disk, you can just reinstall the program from the floppies or CD.

Uninstalling a Program

Programs take up space on the hard disk. At some point you might want to remove a program that you don't use any more to make room for new programs (or for more documents).

To quickly remove a program, open the Control Panel, double-click on the Add/Remove Programs icon, and then click on the Install/Uninstall tab. Highlight the name of the program that you want to remove, then click on the Remove button. The automatic uninstall (if it's available) is safer and more accurate than deleting the program's files or folders yourself.

Installing and Removing Windows 95 Components

When you use the Typical setup to install Windows 95, some components are *not* copied to your hard disk automatically. For instance, components like Briefcase and Microsoft Fax, which don't appeal to every Windows 95 user, are not installed.

The different installation options are discussed in the Appendix.

If you later decide that you do want to use one of those optional components, you can use Windows Setup to add them quickly. Windows Setup also is handy for removing Windows components that you no longer want on disk. Here's how to use it:

1 If you'll be adding components, grab the setup disks or CD-ROM for Windows 95.

2 Go to the Control Panel, double-click on the Add/Remove Programs icon, and then click on the Windows Setup tab to open the dialog box shown in Figure 10.5.

Use Windows Setup to add and remove Windows 95 components.

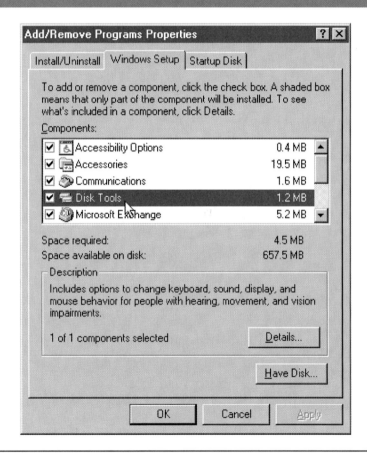

3 As instructed on the screen, select (check) the components to be installed, or retained, on your computer. Clear (deselect) *only* the components to be removed. Answer any prompts that appear. (Be careful not to delete anything you need!)

4 To start the setup, click on OK and follow the instructions.

When the job is done, put the setup disks in a safe place.

The existing check marks show which components are already installed. Do not uncheck a component unless you specifically want to remove that component from your hard disk.

Making a Start-Up Disk

A *start-up disk* allows you to start your computer from a floppy disk on those *very rare* occasions when you can't start Windows from the hard disk (perhaps because the hard disk is damaged). A start-up disk is a must for everyone!

You had a chance to create a start-up disk when you installed Windows 95. But if you didn't create a start-up disk then, or you need an extra one, just follow these steps:

1 Gather your Windows 95 setup disks or CD-ROM.

2 Grab a fresh floppy disk that fits in drive A and label it *Windows 95 Start-Up Disk*. Keep in mind that any information on this disk will be erased completely, so make sure it doesn't contain any important files.

3 Go to the Control Panel, double-click on the Add/Remove Programs icon, and then click on the Startup Disk tab.

4 Click on the Create Disk button and follow the instructions.

5 When the start-up disk is finished, the floppy disk drive will stop making noise and the disk-activity light will

The DOS-like component that comes with Windows 95 supports the /? method of getting help. For example, to get help with the scandisk command, you would type **scandisk /?** and press ⏎ at the DOS command prompt.

stop flashing. Click on OK, then put your setup disks and start-up disk in a safe place.

If you ever need to use the start-up disk, insert it into drive A and restart your computer. When restarting is complete, you'll be at the A:\> DOS prompt. From there, you (or your local computer guru) can use DOS commands to figure out what's wrong.

Tuning Up for Maximum Performance

Computers don't require a lot of maintenance mainly because there are very few moving parts inside the machine. But there is one moving part that's very important: the hard disk that stores all your programs and documents.

A little routine maintenance can keep your hard disk, and hence your entire computer system, running smoothly and at peak performance. In this section, we'll look at some of the routine maintenance tasks that you can perform yourself to keep your system in tip-top shape.

To check available disk space on *any* drive, open My Computer and click on the drive you're interested in. The status bar will show the free space available on that drive.

Checking Your Disk Space

Often it's helpful to know how much space is available on a disk. To find out:

1 Double-click on *My Computer* on the desktop, right-click on the disk icon you're interested in, and choose Properties. Figure 10.6 shows the disk-space pie chart for a floppy disk that is nearly empty.

2 When you're finished viewing the information, choose OK.

FIGURE 10.6

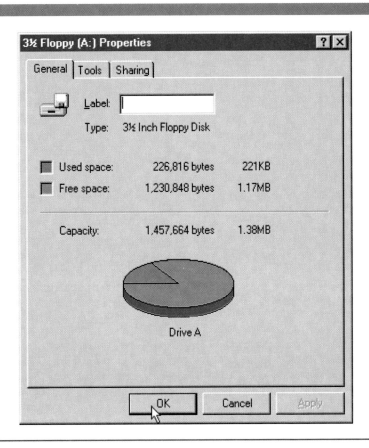

The General Properties for a disk show the amount of free space and used space.

If the disk is relatively empty, you're in good shape. If it's almost full, try the following to make more space available for storing files:

- Delete files you're sure you don't need anymore and then empty the Recycle Bin.

- Remove Windows components and other programs that you no longer need.

- Use ScanDisk to correct errors that may be wasting disk space (see *Scanning Disks for Errors* below).

- As a last resort, use DriveSpace to make more space available (see *Compressing Disks* below).

For a refresher on the Recycle Bin, see Chapter 4.

Defragmenting Your Disks

As you add and delete files, the disk space can become fragmented into small noncontiguous chunks. Although this isn't dangerous, it can slow down the disk and make you wait unnecessarily. To reorganize (defragment) the space on a disk, follow these steps.

① Double-click on *My Computer* on the desktop, right-click on the appropriate disk icon, choose P̲roperties, and click on the Tools tab. The resulting drive Properties dialog box resembles the example shown in Figure 10.7.

FIGURE 10.7

The Properties dialog box for a specific disk drive

This is what you'll see after right-clicking on a disk icon in *My Computer* choosing P̲roperties, and clicking on the Tools tab.

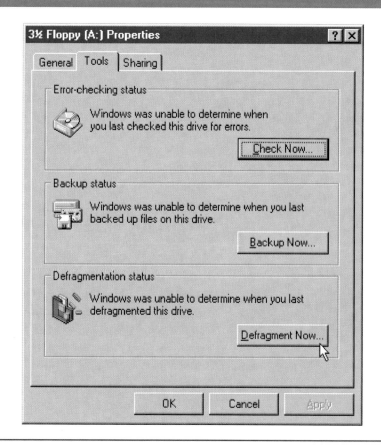

2 Click on <u>D</u>efragment Now to open the Defragmentation dialog box.

3 Click on one of the buttons described below:

<u>S</u>tart Defragments the selected disk.

Select <u>D</u>rive Lets you select another drive to defragment.

<u>A</u>dvanced Lets you choose a different defragmentation method (not usually necessary).

E<u>x</u>it Returns you to the Properties dialog box.

4 When you're finished, choose OK to return to the desktop.

Scanning Disks for Errors

Disks can develop errors that prevent them from storing files properly and running programs correctly. These include such dire-sounding things as cross-linked files, lost file fragments, invalid file names, invalid dates and times, and disk-surface errors. To check for and correct these problems, use ScanDisk frequently. Here's how:

Many things can cause disk errors, but the most common culprit is turning off the computer while it's writing to the disk. Never, ever turn off your computer without choosing Start ➤ Shut<u>d</u>own ➤ <u>Y</u>es first.

1 Double-click on *My Computer* on the desktop, right-click on any disk icon, choose <u>P</u>roperties, and then click on the Tools tab (see Figure 10.7).

2 Click on Check Now to open the ScanDisk dialog box shown in Figure 10.8.

3 In the list at the top, select the drive or drives to be scanned. (To select more than one drive, hold down the Ctrl key while clicking on each drive icon.)

4 In the *Type of test* area, choose the type of test to perform (Stan<u>d</u>ard or <u>T</u>horough). Also choose whether to Automatically <u>f</u>ix errors without prompting.

5 Choose <u>S</u>tart to begin the scan.

FIGURE 10.8

The ScanDisk dialog box

This dialog box lets you choose which disks to scan, how to perform the test, and whether to fix errors automatically.

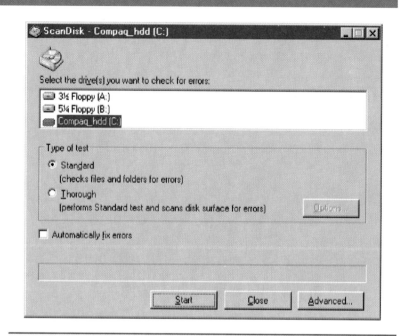

6 Respond to any dialog boxes that appear. When you're finished scanning, choose <u>C</u>lose and OK as needed.

Formatting a Floppy Disk

Windows can store and retrieve files only if the disk is formatted correctly. Formatting functions something like the stripes on a parking lot. *Without* the stripes, drivers have no idea where to park their cars. *With* the stripes, drivers know where to park (though sometimes they ignore the rules and park wherever they please).

Caution! Formatting erases *everything* on the disk. So before you format a floppy disk, find out whether it really needs to be formatted. Simply put the disk into the floppy drive, double-click on *My Computer* on the desktop, then double-click on the drive's icon. If the disk hasn't been formatted, you'll see an error message about the disk not being accessible (to clear this message, click on Cancel). If the disk is formatted, you'll see whatever folders and files it contains.

Buying Floppy Disks

You can buy floppy disks formatted or unformatted. If they're formatted, you don't need to format them again. If they're unformatted, you'll need to format the disks before using them. Formatted disks may cost a little more than unformatted disks, but they're worth it because they save you time.

Here's how to format a floppy disk:

1 Put the disk into drive A or B (as appropriate).

2 Double-click on *My Computer* on the desktop.

3 Right-click on the icon for the floppy disk to be formatted, then choose For<u>m</u>at. A Format dialog box appears in Figure 10.9.

4 You can change the options in the dialog box, though the default choices usually are fine (use the ? button if you need help).

5 To begin formatting the disk, click on <u>S</u>tart.

6 When formatting is complete, click on <u>C</u>lose.

You should format *only* floppy disks that have never been formatted before. Never format a disk that already contains files, unless you are absolutely, positively sure you don't want any of the files on that disk.

FIGURE 10.9

A sample Format dialog box for a 3½" double-sided high-density floppy disk

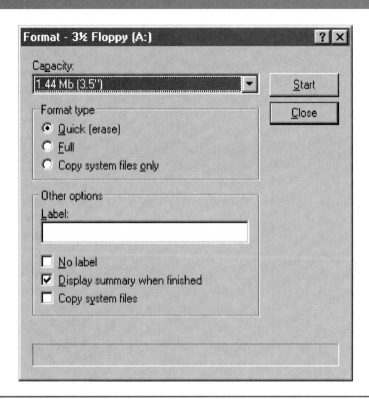

It's not necessary to back up programs often because programs don't really change, and you can always reinstall a program from the original floppy disks or CD. But it *is* important to back up documents that change frequently because otherwise the *only* copy of a document is likely to be the one on your hard disk.

Backing Up Your Files

Backups can protect you when files are lost or damaged because of equipment malfunction, power failure, natural disasters, or operator errors such as deleting files accidentally or making unwanted changes that can't be undone easily. *With* backups, you can restore the lost or damaged files; *without* them, you may lose time and money as you scramble to recreate files from your own memory or from paper records.

Making Backups

The easiest way to back up files from your hard disk is to let the Backup Wizard prompt you through the procedure. Here's how to get started:

1 If you're backing up to floppy disk or tape, gather enough fresh *formatted* disks or tapes to hold the backups.

2 Use either method below to start the Microsoft Backup wizard.

- Double-click on *My Computer* on the desktop. Then right-click on any disk icon, choose Properties, and click on the Tools tab in the dialog box. Finally, click on Backup Now, or

- Choose Start ➤ Programs ➤ Accessories ➤ System Tools ➤ Backup.

3 Let the Wizard step you through the backup procedure.

Follow all the instructions that the wizard presents. When you're done, put your backups in a safe place (fireproof and waterproof, of course) and save them for a rainy day.

Restoring from Backups

Restoring files is pretty much the inverse of backing them up. Of course, you only need to restore files if the originals become lost or damaged. To use restore, gather the backups, then get the Backup Wizard going by following these steps:

1 Click on Start and choose Programs ➤ Accessories ➤ System Tools ➤ Backup.

2 Choose OK twice, then click on the Restore tab.

3 Select the place to Restore From and highlight a Backup Set.

4 Click on Next Step, then check the files and folders to be restored.

If you did a Typical install, Microsoft Backup might not be installed. To install it, follow the steps given earlier in this chapter (see *Installing and Removing Windows 95 Components*).

Microsoft Backup offers many options for the experienced user. You'll find these on the Files, Settings, and Tools menus. For plenty of online Help, choose Help ➤ Help in the Backup menu bar, then click on the Contents tab and double-click on the topic you want.

There are less fancy ways to make backups. For example, you can copy files to floppy disks (see Chapter 4). You also can use file-compression programs—such as PKZIP and PKUNZIP or WinZip (see Chapter 11)—to create and restore backup files. The important thing is to use *some* reliable and regular method to back up your work.

5 Click on Start Restore and respond to any prompts that appear.

When the restoration is finished, click on the OK and Close (X) buttons until you return to the desktop.

Compressing Disks

You can use DriveSpace to compress hard or floppy disks so they contain more free space than the disk originally was designed to hold. DriveSpace also can uncompress disks and adjust the amount of uncompressed space on a disk. Be aware that DriveSpace is an advanced feature that should be used *only* if:

- You've tried other ways to squeeze more space from a disk, such as deleting unwanted files, emptying the Recycle Bin, and removing any space-wasting errors with ScanDisk.

- You cannot afford to buy more disk space.

- You've backed up files on the disk you're about to compress or uncompress. (You'll have a chance to do this when you run DriveSpace.)

Compress at Your Own Risk!

The authors of this book are great believers in the KISS (Keep It Simple, Stupid) approach to computing. Simply stated, the more complicated you make things, the more likely you are to have problems. Using DriveSpace just adds one more level of complexity to the whole system. Disks are fairly cheap these days, so you might want to consider upgrading to a larger hard disk or adding an external hard disk as an alternative to using DriveSpace to cram more stuff on your existing hard disk.

Most people won't need to use DriveSpace, so we'll just tell you how to get started. For more help, start DriveSpace (as explained below), choose <u>H</u>elp ➤ Help <u>T</u>opics from the DriveSpace menu bar, then click on the Contents tab and double-click on the topic you're interested in. Here are the basic steps for using DriveSpace:

1 Choose Start ➤ <u>P</u>rograms ➤ Accessories ➤ System Tools ➤ DriveSpace. The DriveSpace window appears.

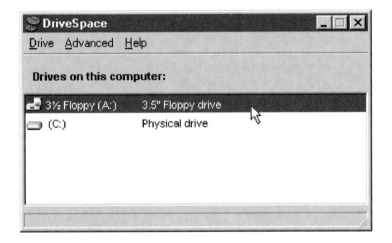

2 Click on the drive you want to work with.

3 Choose one of the options below, depending on what you want to do:

- To determine whether the drive is compressed and to find out how much free and used space it has, choose <u>D</u>rive ➤ <u>P</u>roperties or double-click on the drive icon. Then choose OK to return to the DriveSpace window (see step 2).

- To compress the selected disk (increasing its free space), choose <u>D</u>rive ➤ <u>C</u>ompress from the menu bar, then choose <u>S</u>tart.

Until you're comfort-able with DriveSpace, test these steps on a spare floppy disk rather than your hard disk.

Be sure to back up any files if you haven't done so already.

- To uncompress the selected disk (reducing its free space and making it "normal" again), choose <u>D</u>rive ➤ <u>U</u>ncompress from the menu bar, then choose <u>S</u>tart.

- To adjust the amount of uncompressed space on a compressed drive, choose <u>D</u>rive ➤ Adjust <u>F</u>ree Space, adjust the free space, and choose OK.

4 Carefully follow the instructions that appear and complete any dialog boxes.

Internet, CompuServe, and All That Jazz

Featuring

- Seeing if your modem is ready
- Adding a modem to your PC
- Connecting to America Online
- Connecting to CompuServe
- Surfing the Internet
- Joining the Microsoft Network
- Getting into Bulletin Boards (BBSs)
- Troubleshooting modem problems

You've probably already heard about some of the more popular online services for PCs, such as the Internet, CompuServe, America Online, and the Microsoft Network. In this chapter we'll show you how to connect to those services so you too can start surfing the net. As you'll see, all you need is a modem, an account number, and a PC. (Oh yeah, and some money.)

Seeing if Your Modem Is Ready

You need a modem to connect to any online service. If you have a modem but are not sure whether it's installed, here's an easy way to find out:

1 Click on the Start button and choose <u>S</u>ettings ➤ <u>C</u>ontrol Panel.

2 Double-click on the Modems icon.

3 If you see the Modem Properties dialog box shown in Figure 11.1, and the name of the modem appears to be correct, you're done! Choose Cancel and go straight to the section titled *Using Your Modem* later in this chapter.

FIGURE 11.1

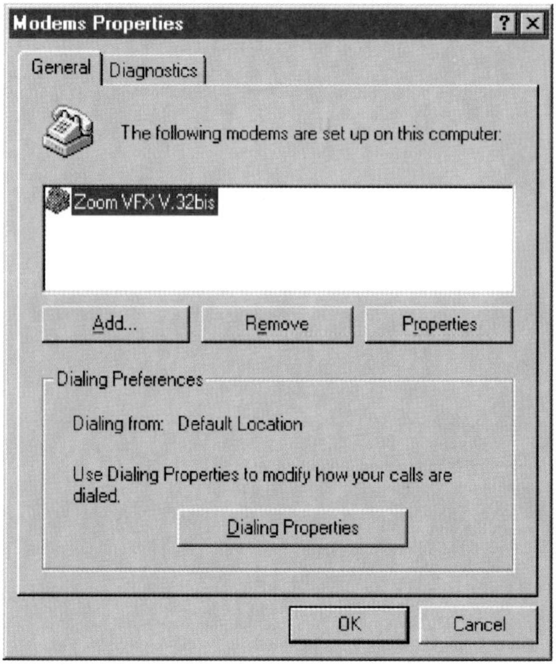

If the Modem Properties dialog box appears and accurately displays the name of your modem, your modem is already installed and ready for use.

Adding a Modem to Your PC

A *modem* is just a gadget that connects your PC to the telephone lines. Many computers come with modems built right in so all you need to do is use a standard telephone cable line to hook the Line plug on the modem to the phone jack on your wall. Optionally, you can hook the phone jack on the modem to your telephone.

If you don't have a modem, you can purchase one from any computer store or mail-order house that advertises in computer magazines. There are three basic models to choose from:

> Internal modem: Fits inside the PC so it doesn't take up any room on your desk. It's a little more complicated to hook up than an external modem, but it doesn't use up the serial port on the back of your computer.
>
> Credit-card-size modem: A credit-card-size modem fits into the PCMCIA slot of a laptop computer (or on a desktop computer that happens to have a PCMCIA slot).
>
> External modem: Hooks into a serial port on the back of your PC. It's easier to install than an internal modem and can easily be moved from one computer to another. However, the computer must have a free serial port.

Most computers have two serial ports, named COM 1 and COM 2 (they're plugs on the back of the system unit). If your mouse is connected to the port labeled COM 1, you can connect the modem to the plug labeled COM 2.

If you do choose to go with an external modem, keep in mind that you'll also need a few cables which may (or may not) come with the modem: (1) a cable to connect the modem to the PC, (2) a cord to connect the modem to the wall jack (and perhaps another to connect the modem to your regular telephone), and perhaps (3) a power cord to plug the modem into a standard wall socket for power.

If you hook a telephone to your modem but do *not* want the modem to answer the phone, you must deactivate the modem's Auto Answer (AA) feature. See your modem manual for instructions.

You might want to go with an external modem if your computer already has a lot of other internal gadgets—like a sound card, CD-ROM, and network card—installed. Adding an internal modem to that already crowded collection of gadgets can be difficult, if not downright impossible!

When choosing a modem, keep in mind that the modem's *top speed*, which is expressed as a *baud rate* or *bps*, is an important factor. The higher the baud rate, the faster the modem can do its job (meaning, the less time you have to wait around for the modem to do something). You should try to get a modem with at least a top speed of 9,600 baud. But if you can afford one that runs at 14.4 (14,400) or 28.8 (28,800) baud, so much the better.

A Note on Fax Modems

A Fax Modem is just a regular modem with the added ability to send documents directly to other fax machines without first printing the document. This a *major* convenience and well worth the small extra cost. All things considered, a 14,400-baud Fax Modem is your best bet in choosing a modem.

Connecting your modem will also be easier if you choose one that is *Windows 95-aware*. To explore an up-to-date list of such modems:

1. Click on the Start button and choose <u>S</u>ettings ➤ <u>C</u>ontrol Panel.

2. Double click on the Modems icon, then click on <u>A</u>dd.

Modems

3. Select (check) the option titled *Don't detect my modem; I will select it from a list.*

4. Click on the Next button. You'll come to the dialog box shown in Figure 11.2.

5. Choose any modem manufacturer's name to see which models are supported by Windows 95.

FIGURE 11.2

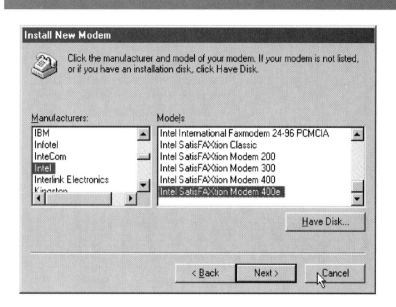

Makes and models of modems supported by Windows 95

If you're just exploring makes and models of supported modems, it's important to cancel out of the dialog box when you're done. You don't want to proceed with the modem installation until you've purchased your modem and connected it to your PC and phone line.

6 After exploring, choose Cancel to back out of the dialog box without making a selection. Then close Control Panel normally.

Installing the Modem

Once you have the modem and appropriate cables in hand, here's how to hook them up to your PC:

1 Set up the modem and connect it to the phone jack. Exactly how you do that depends on what kind of modem you're using:

- If you're just activating an internal modem that's already inside your PC, connect the Line jack on the modem to the phone jack in the wall (and, optionally, connect the Phone jack on the modem to the telephone). Then skip to step 2.

It isn't necessary to connect the modem to the telephone for the modem to work. You really only need to connect the modem to the wall jack. However, if you don't connect the phone to the modem, the phone won't ring on incoming calls, nor will you get a dial tone when you pick up the receiver.

- If you're using a credit-card-size modem, follow the instructions for inserting the modem in the PCMCIA slot and hooking it to the phone jack. Then go to step 2.

- If you are installing your own internal modem, *shut down Windows, turn off everything,* and install the modem per the manufacturer's instructions. Be sure to connect the line jack on the modem to the phone jack in the wall. When you've finished and reassembled your computer, turn the PC back on to get to the Windows 95 desktop, then head straight to step 2 below.

- If you are installing an external modem, shut down Windows 95; turn off everything; and connect the modem to the PC, phone jack, and wall socket as instructed by the manufacturer. Then turn everything (including the modem) back on. When you get to the Windows 95 desktop, move on to step 2 below.

2 In Windows 95, click on the Start button and choose Settings ➤ Control Panel.

3 Double-click on the Modems icon, then click on the Add button.

4 If (and *only* if) the *Don't detect my modem; I will select it from a list* option is selected, click on it once to clear the check mark.

5 Click on the Next button and follow the instructions on the screen.

If Windows 95 can detect your modem, it will automatically be installed to use the highest speed possible, with the universal modem settings of N81 (no parity, 8 data bits, 1 stop bit). You need not change those settings—just close the dialog box(es) to work your way back to the desktop.

If Windows 95 cannot detect your modem, you'll need to perform steps 1 through 3, select the *Don't detect my modem; I will select it from a list* option, then choose the modem (or one of the *Standard Modem Types* options from the list) and proceed from there.

Using Your Modem

Once your modem is installed, there are many ways to use it. The general procedure is:

1 Make sure the modem is connected to the telephone wall jack.

2 If you have an external modem, make sure it's plugged in and turned on.

● If you want to connect to one of the online services for which you have an account, start the appropriate program on your PC, as discussed later in this chapter.

If you have any problems using your modem, see the Troubleshooting section near the end of this chapter.

About Zipped Files

When you're downloading files (copying files from) any service, you're likely to come across files with the exten- sion .zip. These *zipped* files, as they're called, are compressed to make the transfer go more quickly. Before you can open or use such a file, you need to *unzip* it, using the PKUNZIP program. You can download a copy of PKUNZIP from most services (and BBSs), or you can order a copy (for about twenty-five bucks) from PKWARE, Inc., 7545 N. Port Washington Rd., Glendale, WI 53217.

Another program that makes zipping and unzipping a breeze is WinZip for Windows 95 ($29, including postage). To order by credit card, call PsL at (800) 242-4775 or fax your credit card and ordering info to (713) 524-6398. To order by mail, send a check to Nico Mak Computing, Inc., PO Box 919, Bristol, CT 06011. To order WinZip on CompuServe, type go swreg and order product #402.

- If you want to connect to a Bulletin Board System (BBS), use HyperTerminal, as discussed later in this chapter.

- If your modem is hooked to your voice phone, you can use the Windows 95 Phone Dialer (see Chapter 8) to dial frequently called numbers.

Connecting to America Online

America Online is one of the friendliest online services available. Their monthly service charge and connect-time charges are also very reasonable. Before you connect to America Online, you'll need to purchase the America Online software kit for Windows (available at most computer stores) and register as a member, or you can contact America Online at:

> 8619 Westwood Center Dr.
> Vienna, VA 22182-2285
> (703)447-8700

You'll receive the appropriate software, instructions for installing it, and information on monthly and connect-time charges.

When you receive the software, install it on your computer as described in the instructions that come with the software. Once you've done that, connecting to America Online is a piece of cake. Start the Windows America Online program as you would any other program: by double-clicking on its icon (which will be labeled WAOL or something similar) or by choosing it from the appropriate Start ➤ Programs menu. You'll be taken to a screen like the one shown in Figure 11.3.

When you get connected, let us know how you're doing. Choose M̲ail ➤ Compose mail and drop us a line at SimpsonAC

Type in your password and click on the Sign On button. Once you're connected you can use the menu bar, toolbar, and additional icons and buttons that appear on the screen to explore the service. When you're ready to disconnect, just choose F̲ile ➤ E̲xit ➤ Exit Application from the menu bar.

FIGURE 11.3

The WAOL (Windows America Online) program makes it easy to connect to and get around in America Online.

Connecting to CompuServe

CompuServe is also a popular service for PC users and is especially well liked for its electronic-mail services and its ability to send files from one PC to another.

You can purchase CompuServe software and registration packets from most computer stores, or you can contact CompuServe directly at:

> CompuServe Information Service
> 5000 Arlington Centre Blvd.
> P.O. Box 20212
> Columbus, OH 43220-9988

Phone numbers (voice) are:

United States	(800)524-3388
UK	0800-289-378
Germany	0130-37-32
other European countries	44-272-255-111

When you get your software (named WinCIM for Windows CompuServe Information Manager), install it per the instructions that come with the program. You'll also receive an account ID, password, and an explanation of the charges for your connect time.

To try out e-mail, choose Mail ➤ Create Mail. Then drop us a line at the Sybex Publishing Forum (choose Services ➤ Go, type **sybex**, and then click on OK) and see what all the authors are up to.

Once you get the WinCIM program installed, connecting is easy. Start the WinCIM program by double-clicking on its icon or by choosing it from the appropriate Start ➤ Programs menus. You'll be taken to a screen similar to the one shown in Figure 11.4. Choose a service by clicking (e.g., click on the Basic Services icon) or by choosing a service from the WinCIM menu bar (e.g., choose Mail ➤ Get New Mail). Once you're connected, use the menu bar, toolbar, and other prompts on the screen to learn more about CompuServe and explore your options. When you're ready to disconnect, click on the toolbar's Exit button or choose File ➤ Exit from WinCIM's menu bar.

FIGURE 11.4

The WinCIM program gives you an easy way to connect to and navigate through the CompuServe Information Service (CIS).

Surfing the Internet

The Internet is a gigantic network of computers and information services that spans the globe. Internet does *not* rate very high on the user-friendly scale. If you don't want to spend several days or weeks learning all the ins and outs of the Internet, you can limit yourself to e-mail or other popular features by *tapping in* from your CompuServe, America Online, or Microsoft Network program. When you're in one of those services, search the online help for *Internet* to see what's possible.

To access all that the Internet has to offer, you can buy a book and software kit at a reasonable price. We use NetCruiser (see Figure 11.5), which comes free with the book titled *Access the Internet!* (Sybex, 1995).

When you want to sign off, choose File ➤ Exit from NetCruiser's (or whatever program you're using) menu bar.

You may have heard that the Internet is free of charge, but that's only partially true. Some services are free, but your Internet provider (the company that hooks you into the Internet) will almost certainly charge you for connect time.

FIGURE 11.5

NetCruiser is just one of many programs that provides Windows access to the Internet.

When we say the Internet is huge, we mean *really* huge. A list of topics that *aren't* covered somewhere on the Internet would be shorter than a list of topics that *are* covered—but we can't even think of *one* topic that isn't discussed at some length *somewhere* on the net. That is to say, the net is just too big a topic to discuss here.

You also can set up The Microsoft Network by double-clicking on the *Set Up The Microsoft Network* icon if it's available on your Windows 95 desktop.

Then buy a book that's just about the Internet! Try *The Internet Roadmap* (Sybex, 1994) or *Access the Internet!* (Sybex, 1995).

Joining the Microsoft Network

The Microsoft Network (MSN) definitely earns the user-friendly (and fun) rating for information services. Chances are you already have an icon for Microsoft Network right on your desktop. If so, just make sure your modem is hooked up and turned on, then double-click on *The Microsoft Network* icon to try it out.

If you can't find an icon for the Microsoft Network on your Windows 95 desktop, perhaps the program isn't installed yet. To install it, follow these steps:

1 Gather up your original Windows 95 installation disks or CD. Put floppy disk 1 in drive A or B, or put the CD in your CD-ROM drive.

2 Click on the Start button and choose Settings ➤ Control Panel.

3 Double-click on Add/Remove Programs.

4 Click on the Windows Setup tab. Then...

- If the *The Microsoft Network* option is *not* already checked, select it and go to step 5.

- If the *The Microsoft Network* option is already checked, the program is probably installed, but you need to set up an account. Choose Cancel, close the Control Panel, and go to the section titled *Signing Up for the Microsoft Network* below.

5 Choose OK and follow any instructions that appear on the screen. Close the Control Panel when you're done.

Now you'll need to sign up for the network, as discussed next.

Signing Up for the Microsoft Network

To sign up as a member of the Microsoft Network, follow these steps:

1. Double-click on the The Microsoft Network icon on your Windows 95 desktop or click on the Start button and choose Programs ➤ The Microsoft Network.

2. Follow the sign-up instructions on the screen.

You need sign up only once, not every time you want to connect.

Once you're signed up, double-clicking on The Microsoft Network on your desktop will take you to the Sign In dialog box. Fill in your Member ID and Password and then click on Connect. In a few moments, your screen will resemble the example shown in Figure 11.6. Feel free to explore at your own pace (you can even use Start ➤ Find ➤ On the Microsoft Network to find things on the network). When you're ready to disconnect, click on the Close (X) button (or press Alt+F4) until you're asked whether it's OK to disconnect; then click on Yes.

FIGURE 11.6

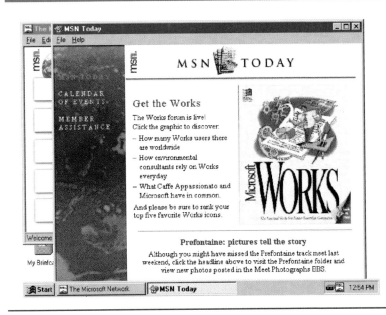

Your screen will look something like this when you've connected to the Microsoft Network.

Not *all* small bulletin board services are free. But you'll usually know if one charges money because (1) they'll ask for credit-card info the minute you log in, or (2) they'll use a 900 number that charges for your connect time.

We know you have HyperTerminal because it comes with Windows 95! But you may need to install this Accessories program (see Chapter 10).

Getting into Bulletin Boards (BBSs)

In addition to the big online services discussed in the preceding sections, there are thousands of smaller bulletin board systems that you can tap into. Many computer clubs, computer stores, and enthusiastic individuals provide free programs, help, and other services on these small independent BBSs.

Unlike the big services, you generally *don't* need special software or an account number to tap into one of these services. Just dial in and follow the instructions on the screen. All you need is a modem and the HyperTerminal program that comes with Windows 95.

Most BBSs advertise in small local computer publications. When you see an ad for a BBS, it might show information like this:

The ChatterBox BBS..............555-1234 9600 8N1

The *555-1234* part is the phone number and the *9600 8N1* represents the settings you need to use in HyperTerminal to make the connection. Here's how to do that:

1 Make sure your modem is connected to the phone jack (if it's an external modem, make sure it's plugged in and turned on).

2 Click on the Start button and choose <u>P</u>rograms ➤ Accessories ➤ HyperTerminal.

3 Double-click on the Hypertrm icon.

4 In the Connection Description dialog box that appears, enter the name of the BBS and choose whatever icon tickles your fancy (see Figure 11.7). Then choose OK.

5 In the next dialog box, type in the phone number of the BBS (see Figure 11.8). If you've already installed the modem, as described earlier in this chapter, the other information in the dialog box will already be filled in for you. Choose OK.

FIGURE 11.7

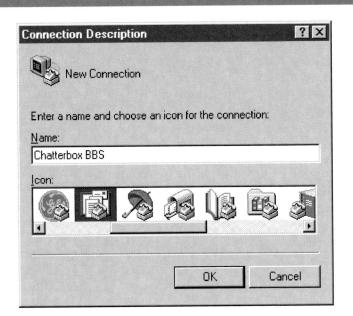

The Connection Description dialog box

This dialog box lets you pick the name and an icon for a bulletin board service.

FIGURE 11.8

Fill in the phone number of the BBS. If you've already installed your modem, the rest of the information will be filled in.

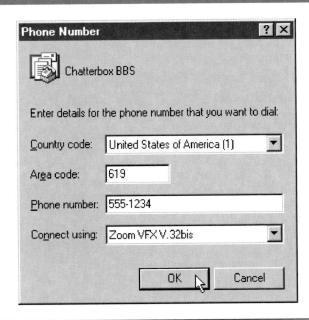

6 After you choose OK, the Connect dialog box will appear. Choose <u>D</u>ial to make the connection.

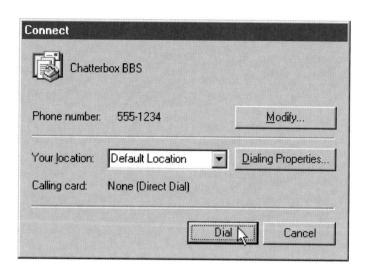

You should hear some activity as your modem makes the connection; things will quiet down once the connection is made. On many bulletin board systems, you need to press ↵ once or twice after the modem quiets down to make the connection. When you're connected, the BBS will probably start asking you questions, as shown in Figure 11.9. Type in your response to each question and press ↵.

Eventually you'll come to a screen that explains how to navigate and how to log off when you're done. Be sure to log off when you've completed your session.

To log off a BBS, usually you type **g**↵, choose <u>C</u>all ➤ <u>D</u>isconnect, then choose <u>F</u>ile ➤ E<u>x</u>it from HyperTerminal's menu bar.

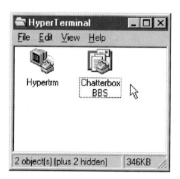

In the future, you need not go through all this rigmarole to reconnect to that same BBS. Instead, click on the Start button, choose Accessories ➤ HyperTerminal, and double-click on the icon for the BBS.

FIGURE 11.9

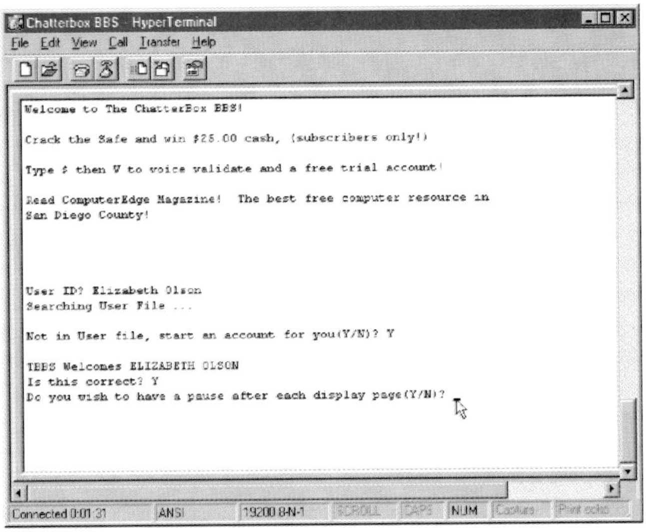

Success! We've connected to the Chatterbox BBS.

Troubleshooting Modem Problems

If you have any problems at all using your modem, let Windows 95 help you troubleshoot the problem:

1 Click on the Start button and choose <u>H</u>elp.

2 Click on the Contents tab, then double-click on Troubleshooting to open that book. Then double-click on *If you have trouble using your modem*.

3 Follow the instructions and make your selections from the dialog boxes that appear.

In this chapter, you've learned how to connect your modem and hop onto the information superhighway's many online services. In the next chapter you'll learn how to share printers, files, programs, and other resources on a local-area network (LAN).

CHAPTER 12

Sharing Resources on a LAN

Featuring

● Signing onto the network
● How to share a printer
● How to share folders
● How to share programs
● How to share a CD-ROM drive
● Signing off of the network
● Network tips

If your computer is connected to a local-area network (LAN), you can share resources with other computers on that LAN. Before we go any further with that, let us just say that in this book we're assuming your job is *not* to create the LAN. Rather, somebody with the appropriate expertise has already done that for you. But now that the LAN is working, you want to take advantage of the many conveniences it offers. For example, you might want to use a printer that's connected to someone else's PC. Or you may want to open and edit documents that are in a folder on someone else's PC.

Signing On to the Network

If your computer is on a network, you'll probably need to sign on to the network whenever you first start Windows. You'll see one of these dialog boxes.

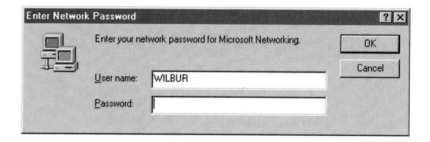

If the User name line is blank or not your user name, type in your user name. Then type in your password (it will appear only as asterisks to prevent someone from peeking over your shoulder and discovering your password) and choose OK. If this is the first time you've logged on with this password, you may see some additional prompts on the screen. Just follow the directions that appear.

Identifying Your Computer

You may want to assign, or change, your computer's name, workgroup, description, or other characteristics:

1. Choose Start ➤ Settings ➤ Control Panel, double-click on Network, and click on the Identification tab (see Figure 12.1).

2. As necessary, change the Computer name, Workgroup, and Computer Description.

3. Optionally, choose another tab and change whatever settings seem appropriate (press F1 or use the ? button to get help).

4. When you've finished, choose OK and follow any instructions that appear on the screen.

Only PCs that are on the LAN *and* have the same Workgroup name can share resources. If you change the Workgroup, you'll no longer have access to computers from your old Workgroup.

How to Share a Printer

In the next two sections we'll show you how to share a printer on the LAN. As you'll see, the first step is to make the printer available to LAN members.

FIGURE 12.1

The Network dialog box with the Identification tab selected

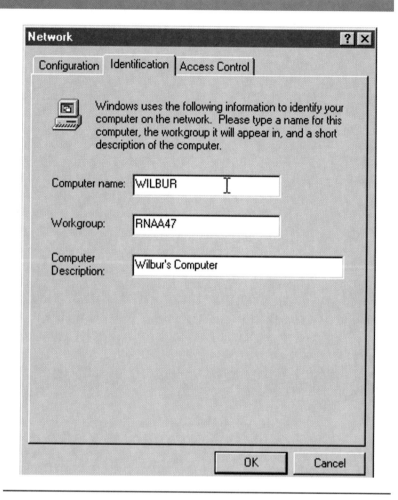

On the PC That Has the Printer Attached...

Before others on the LAN can use a printer, the person who has the printer on his or her PC must *share* the printer. Here's how:

① On the computer that has the printer attached to it, make sure the printer is turned on, connected, and installed for use in Windows 95. If you're not sure whether the printer is installed, click on the Start button and choose Settings ➤ Printers. If you *don't* see an icon for the printer, double-click on Add Printer and follow the instructions on the screen until the installation is complete.

In the user's guide, look up *network* in the index and follow any instructions provided.

2 You might want to quickly check the user's guide that came with the printer to see if there is anything special you need to do to make the printer work on a network.

3 Next, make sure the PC is prepared to share its printer. Click on the Start button and choose Settings ➤ Control Panel. Double-click on the Network icon, click on the Configuration tab, and then click on the File and Print Sharing button. If the option to share the printer is *not* selected, select it as shown below. Then choose OK and follow any instructions that appear on the screen.

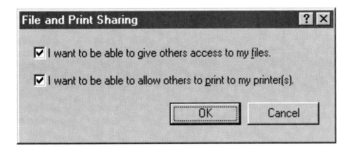

4 Now, to share the printer, click on the Start button and choose Settings ➤ Control Panel. Then double-click on the Printers icon.

Printers

5 Next, click on the printer that you want to share so its icon is selected, as in the example of the HP LaserJet III printer shown at right.

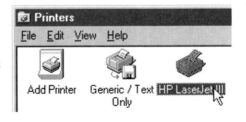

Remember, you can press Fl or use the ? button for help.

6 Choose File ➤ Sharing from the Printers dialog box's menu bar. Click on the Sharing tab, choose Shared As, and enter a brief share name and comment, as shown in Figure 12.2. If you want to limit access to the printer to users that know some password, you can also add a password.

7 You can choose additional settings from the General and Details tabs, though it's not necessary to do so.

8 Choose OK, then close the Control Panel.

The printer is now available to other PCs on the LAN.

FIGURE 12.2

The HP LaserJet III printer on Wilbur's PC will be shared as "HP Laserjet."

HP LaserJet III Properties   [?][X]

| Graphics | Fonts | Device Options |
| General | Details | Sharing | Paper |

○ Not Shared

◉ Shared As:

Share Name: [HP Laserjet]

Comment: [HP Laserjet III on Wilbur's PC]

Password: [   ]

[OK]   [Cancel]   [Apply]

On a PC That Wants Access to the Shared Printer...

Now you need to make the other PC(s) aware that the printer is available. Follow these steps:

1 Go to any PC on the LAN that needs to use the shared printer.

2 Click on the Start button and choose Settings ➤ Printers.

3 Double-click on Add Printer, read the text, and choose Next from the first Wizard dialog box.

4 Choose Network Printer, then click on Next.

5 In the next Wizard dialog box, choose the Browse button. In the Browse for Printer dialog box, double-click on the name of the computer that has the printer attached (Wilbur in this example), then click on the name of the printer to share, as shown in Figure 12.3.

6 Select OK, then choose Next, and follow all instructions on the screen to complete the installation.

Using the Shared Printer

Once you've completed the above steps, you can use the shared printer at any time just as if it were connected to your own PC. If the name of the printer shown is not the shared printer, select the shared printer using the Printer button, or Select Printer button, or whatever button is available in that program.

Some programs might require that you go through Page Setup, rather than Print, to choose a printer. For example, in WordPad if you choose File ➤ Page Setup and then click on

In most programs you can choose File ➤ Print to get to that program's print dialog box.

FIGURE 12.3

Here we've chosen "hp laserjet" on Wilbur as the printer we want to use.

the <u>P</u>rinter button, you'll be taken to the dialog box shown in Figure 12.4, where you can select the shared printer.

Troubleshooting Shared Printer Problems

If you have trouble printing to a shared printer:

- First make sure the printer is turned on and online and the PC that it's physically connected to is also turned on and running Windows.

- If the problem persists, go to the PC from which you are trying to print, click on Start, choose <u>H</u>elp ➤

FIGURE 12.4

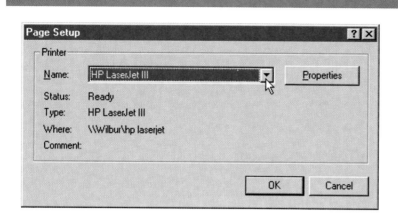

Specifying the printer on Wilbur's computer after choosing File ➤ Page Setup in WordPad

Contents, double-click on Troubleshooting, and choose *If you have trouble printing.*

● If neither of those things work, check the printer's user's guide for information on using that printer on a network.

How to Share Folders

Sharing folders on a LAN is simple once the LAN is up and running. When you share a folder, other members of the LAN can access that folder as though it were on their own hard disk. The other members can also save files to that shared folder.

If the shared folder contains still other folders, those sub-folders are also available to the other LAN members.

On the PC That Contains the Folder to Share...

Let's say that Wilbur's PC has a modem and a folder named *Recent Downloads* where he stores files that he has recently downloaded from the Internet or some other service. Hanley

If PCs on your network are running Windows 3.11 for Workgroups, you can use File Manager's Disk ➤ Share As command to share the Windows 3.11 drives and directories. You also can use File Manager's Disk ➤ Connect Network Drive command to connect (*map*) Windows 3.11 drives to shareable drives and directories on networked computers. For details, look up *File Manager* in your Windows 3.11 documentation or use File Manager's online Help.

wants access to the files in that folder. The first step to giving that access to Hanley would be for Wilbur to *share* his directory by following these steps:

1 On the PC that has the folder to be shared (Wilbur's, in this example), first make sure the PC is prepared to share folders, as detailed earlier in the chapter.

2 Open (double-click on) My Computer.

3 Work your way to the folder to be shared and click on it once to make sure it's selected (highlighted). For example, in Figure 12.5 we've selected the folder named *Recent Downloads*.

4 From the menu bar in the window that contains the selected folder, choose File ➤ Sharing.

5 Choose Shared As, enter a brief share name and comment, and choose attributes as shown in Figure 12.6 (press F1 or use the Help (?) button if you need help).

FIGURE 12.5

The folder named "Recent Downloads" is selected.

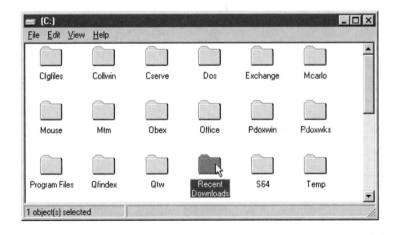

FIGURE 12.6

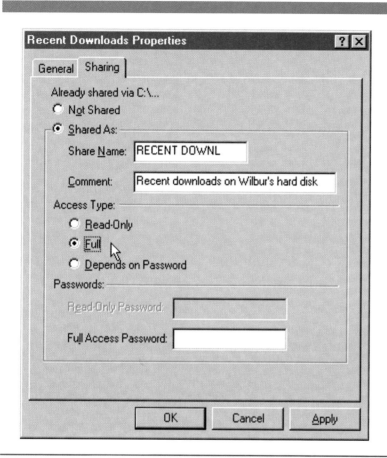

The Sharing dialog box for the folder

The folder named *Recent Downloads* will be shared on the network, under the name RECENT DOWNL, with full read/write access.

6 Choose OK. When you return to the previous window, the shared folder will have a little hand under it to indicate that it is a shared folder.

Recent Downloads

That's it for sharing—Wilbur can now go about his business normally. The shared folder and all of its contents are now available to other members of the LAN. Let's see how Hanley can access the files in that folder from his PC.

Mapping a drive letter to a shared folder is just a way to refer to a shared folder on someone else's PC with a short name. For example, rather than referring to a shared folder as \\Wilburs_pc\ marketing\ customers, you can refer to it as though it were a disk drive, such as M:.

On a PC That Wants Access to the Shared Folder...

The most convenient way to access a shared folder on the LAN is to *map a drive* letter to the shared folder and also have the shared folder automatically reconnect every time you log onto the LAN. Here's how to do it:

1 Go to the PC from which you want to access the shared folder.

2 Open (double-click on) Network Neighborhood.

What Network Neighborhood Shows

Network Neighborhood works like My Computer, only it's not limited to folders (and printers) that are on your particular PC. Instead, it shows all the shared resources to which you have access on the LAN.

You might notice an icon labeled Entire Network in Network Neighborhood. Opening that option shows shared resources on all the workgroups on the LAN. In this book, we're assuming the LAN is pretty small (and all PCs are in the same workgroup), so we won't discuss the Entire Network options in any more detail.

3 Double-click on the name of the PC that contains the shared directory, then click on the name of the shared folder that you want to connect to, as shown in Figure 12.7.

4 From the menu bar in the window that contains the selected folder, choose File ➤ Map Network Drive.

FIGURE 12.7

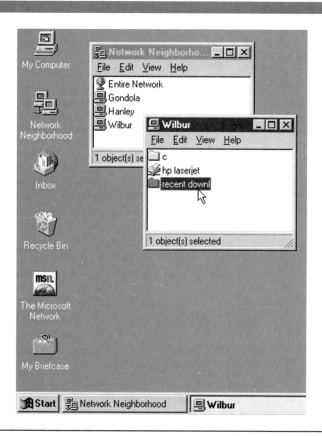

The shared folder named 'recent downl" on Wilbur's PC, selected via Network Neighborhood

5 In the dialog box that appears, choose any available drive letter and, if you want to automatically reconnect to this directory at future log-ons, choose the *Reconnect at logon* option.

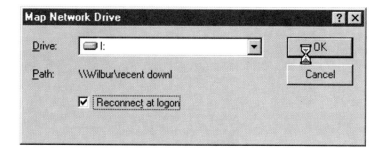

Drive letters A and B are reserved for your local floppy drives. Drive C is your hard disk. Any additional drives, such as a CD-ROM, will be named D, E, and so forth. Don't use the reserved drive letters to identify mapped network drives.

6 Choose OK, then close the open windows.

Using the Shared Folder

Once you've mapped a drive letter to the shared folder, it acts like a regular drive that's attached to your PC. For example:

● When browsing your PC via My Computer or Windows Explorer, the shared folder appears as a network drive in the list of folders and drives.

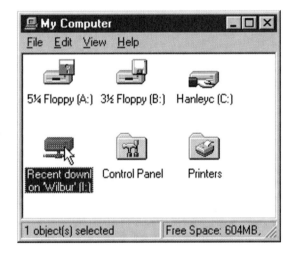

If you have *not* mapped a drive letter to a shared folder, the only way to get to that folder is via Network Neighborhood, as discussed in steps 2 and 3 earlier in this section. But once you're in that folder, you can move and copy files using the standard dragging techniques or options on the File menu.

● When you choose File ➤ Open from a program's menu bar, you can click on the Drives or *Look in* option and choose the shared folder's drive letter to view files (and other folders) within that shared folder.

● Likewise, when you choose File ➤ Save, File ➤ Save As, File ➤ Close, or File ➤ Exit in a program and you have not already saved the document you're working on, you can choose the shared folder's drive letter from the

Drives (or *Save in*) list to save your document to the shared folder.

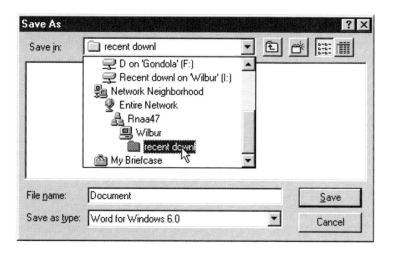

How to Share Programs

You can share programs by sharing the folders that contain those programs. Let's suppose Hanley has a collection of game programs named *FunGames* on his hard disk. Wilbur can't fit all those programs on his hard disk, but he'd like to run some of the games on his PC (in his spare time). To let Wilbur use the games, Hanley first must share the folder containing the FunGames programs from his PC.

Suppose Wilbur wants to run *TimeTravl* (a program in the FunGames collection) on his PC. Here's what he must do:

1 Map a drive (perhaps M) to the shared folder on Hanley's PC. When he maps the drive, Windows automatically opens the shared *FunGames* folder.

2 Open the folder that contains TimeTravl's start-up icon (this folder is named *TimeTravl*).

Many programs—especially suites such as Microsoft Office and Novell PerfectOffice—require

special licenses and installation procedures to run on networked computers. If in doubt, look up *networks* in the documentation for the program you want to share.

3   Find the icon to launch that program (*TimeTravl* or *TimeTravl.exe*) and drag that icon from its window onto Wilbur's desktop, as shown in Figure 12.8.

Wilbur can repeat this process to create similar shortcuts to other FunGames programs. When he's done making shortcuts, Wilbur can close any open windows.

To run a FunGames program from his PC, Wilbur double-clicks on its shortcut icon on his PC's desktop. Windows then copies the appropriate program from the shared folder on Hanley's PC into the memory on Wilbur's PC and runs the program normally!

FIGURE 12.8

Wilbur mapped drive M to Hanley's shared "FunGames" folder. Next, he opened the "TimeTravl" folder within "FunGames" on Hanley's PC to find the icon for "TimeTravl." Then he created a shortcut to the TimeTravl program by dragging that icon to his desktop.

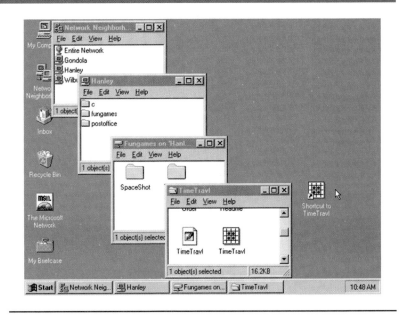

How to Share a CD-ROM Drive

Sharing a CD can be a little tricky because the contents of the CD-ROM drive can change. But if Wilbur shares his CD-ROM drive, Hanley can use Network Neighborhood on his PC to see what CD is in Wilbur's drive and optionally copy files from, or run programs on, that CD. Here's how:

● Wilbur must first share the entire CD-ROM drive. To do that, he opens My Computer, clicks on the icon for the CD-ROM drive, and chooses <u>F</u>ile ➤ S<u>h</u>aring.

● Now he chooses <u>S</u>hared As and fills in the appropriate boxes as shown below.

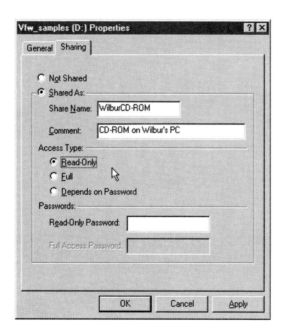

We chose <u>R</u>ead Only as the Access Type for the CD-ROM drive because (virtually) all CD-ROM drives are read-only anyway. In fact, the ROM in CD-ROM stands for Read-Only Memory.

● When Hanley wants to take a peek at what's in Wilbur's CD-ROM, he opens Network Neighborhood on his PC, opens the icon for Wilbur, and then opens the icon for wilburcd-rom as shown in Figure 12.9.

FIGURE 12.9

Using Network Neighborhood, Hanley has opened the CD-ROM drive on Wilbur's PC and can now see the folders on the CD in that drive.

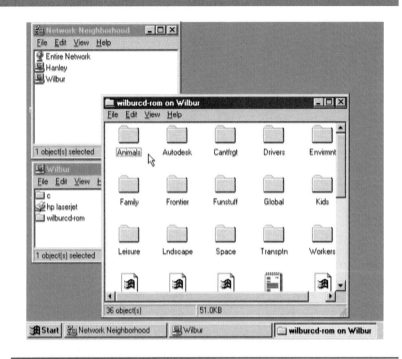

If Wilbur *does* switch to another CD, Hanley simply needs to go through Network Neighborhood on his PC again to see what's on the current CD.

When the wilburcd-rom window opens, it displays the names of the folders and files on the CD that's currently in Wilbur's CD-ROM drive. Now Hanley can copy files from the CD to his own computer or run programs on the CD as long as Wilbur doesn't switch to another CD.

Signing Off of the Network

If you're going to be away from your PC for a while and don't want another user to go traipsing through the network under your user name and password, you should sign off without shutting down the PC:

1 Click on the Start button and choose Sh<u>u</u>tdown.

2 Choose _Close all programs and log on as a different user?_, then choose Yes.

Other users can still log on through your PC. But as long as they don't know your password, they can't assume your identity on the network.

Network Tips

What we've covered in this chapter may take care of everything you ever need to do on a LAN. But there is much more that you can explore—far more than we can cover in one small introductory Windows 95 book. If you want to explore more topics, try using your online documentation:

1 Click on the Start button and choose Help.

2 Click on the Contents tab.

3 Double-click on the How To... book, then double-click on the Use a Network book and read whatever topics interest you.

4 You might also want to explore topics under the headings of _share_, _sharing_, and _passwords_.

Click on the Index tab in Help and search for appropriate topics.

This chapter has covered the essentials of sharing resources on a local-area network. In the next chapter we'll focus on Microsoft Exchange and similar programs that provide a central place for managing local e-mail, wide-area network e-mail, and faxing.

CHAPTER 13

Using Microsoft Exchange

Featuring

- Preparing for Microsoft Exchange
- Setting up Microsoft Exchange
- Changing Exchange profiles
- Using Microsoft Exchange
- Getting the most from Microsoft Exchange

Microsoft Exchange is a central clearinghouse for all your PC communications, including e-mail from your local-area network and/or services like The Microsoft Network. If you have a fax modem installed on your computer, you can also use Exchange to send and receive faxes.

In this chapter, we'll focus on getting Exchange set up on your PC. Then we'll provide general instructions for sending and receiving messages with Exchange.

Preparing for Microsoft Exchange

Microsoft Exchange lets you manage four types of electronic communications:

Fax: To use Microsoft Exchange for sending (and receiving) faxes, you must first install a modem as discussed at the start of Chapter 11.

Microsoft Network Mail: If you've signed up for The Microsoft Network (Chapter 11), you can use Microsoft Exchange to manage your e-mail from that service.

Local E-Mail: To use Microsoft Exchange to manage e-mail on a local-area network (LAN), you must be on a LAN. The person responsible for setting up the LAN will need to set up local e-mail and give you an address and password.

Setting Up Microsoft Exchange

Step one in setting up Microsoft Exchange is to make sure it has been installed on your PC. If Exchange *has* been installed, you'll see the *Inbox* icon on the Windows 95 desktop. In that case, you can skip to *Using Microsoft Exchange*. Otherwise, you'll need to install Exchange on the PC as discussed in the next section.

Installing Exchange

If Exchange isn't already on your PC, follow these steps to install it:

1 Gather up your original Windows 95 disks or CD.

2 Click on the Start button and choose <u>S</u>ettings ➤ <u>C</u>ontrol Panel.

3 Double-click on the Add/Remove Programs icon, then click on the Windows Setup tab.

4 Select (check) the Microsoft Exchange icon. If you're planning to use Exchange to manage faxes, select the Microsoft Fax icon as well, as shown below.

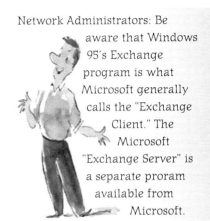

Network Administrators: Be aware that Windows 95's Exchange program is what Microsoft generally calls the "Exchange Client." The Microsoft "Exchange Server" is a separate proram available from Microsoft.

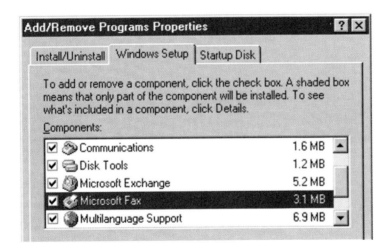

5 Choose OK and follow the instructions on the screen.

When you're done, you'll be taken to the Microsoft Exchange Setup Wizard, where you can define the services you want Exchange to manage. Just follow the instructions on the screen. If you're not sure what option is best, take the Wizard's suggestion. Don't worry if you make a mistake: You can always go back and add, change, or delete options later using the methods discussed next.

Changing Exchange Profiles

Once you've installed Exchange, you may never need to change the settings (or *profiles*) for the messaging services. But if you do, it's easy enough. Here's how:

If you've already started Exchange, you can update the service settings by choosing Tools ➤ Services.

1 Click on the Start button, choose Settings ➤ Control Panel, and then double-click on the *Mail and Fax* icon. Or, right-click on the Inbox icon on your desktop and choose Properties.

2 If no profiles have been set up yet, you will see the Microsoft Exchange Profiles dialog box shown in Figure 13.1 (you can also get to this dialog box by clicking on the Show Profiles button shown in Figure 13.2). Here's what you can do in the Microsoft Exchange Profiles dialog box:

● To add a new profile, click on the Add button and let the Inbox Setup Wizard guide you through

---

FIGURE 13.1

This dialog box appears if either you haven't set up any profiles or you've clicked on the Show Profiles button in the Properties dialog box shown in Figure 13.2.

Microsoft Exchange Profiles   ☒

General

The following profiles are set up on this computer:

MS Exchange Settings

Add...   Remove   Properties   Copy...

When starting Microsoft Exchange, use this profile:

MS Exchange Settings

Close   Cancel   Apply   Help

setting up the information services you want to use with Microsoft Exchange. When you're finished, click on Finish. You'll be returned to the Microsoft Exchange Profiles dialog box.

- To delete or copy an existing profile, click on the profile name you want to use, then click on the Remove button (to delete that profile) or the Copy button (to copy that profile to a new name). Answer the prompts that appear.

- Choose a default profile from the *When starting Microsoft Exchange, use this profile* drop-down list.

- To change the properties of an existing profile, click on the profile you want to change and then click on the Properties button. You'll be taken to the dialog box shown in Figure 13.2.

If a profile already exists and you just want to add a new service, *do not* use the Add button in the Microsoft Exchange Profiles dialog box. Instead, go to the Properties dialog box shown in Figure 13.2 and use its Add button to add the new service.

FIGURE 13.2

This dialog box lets you change the settings for the currently selected profile.

MS Exchange Settings Properties

Services | Delivery | Addressing

The following information services are set up in this profile:

Microsoft Fax
Microsoft Mail
Personal Address Book
Personal Folders
The Microsoft Network Online Service

Add...   Remove   Properties

Copy...   About...

Show Profiles...

OK   Cancel   Apply   Help

Generally, you'll only need to change the Services tab's options, so we'll stick with those options here.

3 If you see a dialog box similar to the one in Figure 13.2, you can change the properties of the currently selected profile (usually named MS Exchange Settings).

- To add a new service to the profile, click on the A_dd button, choose an information service from the list, click on OK, and fill in the dialog boxes that appear.

- To delete an existing service or copy it to another profile, click on the service name and then click on the R_emove or Cop_y button, as appropriate.

- To change the properties of an existing service, click on the service name and then click on the P_roperties button. Update the dialog box as necessary and choose OK when you're done.

4 When you've finished updating the profiles and services, choose OK and Close as needed.

Using Microsoft Exchange

Once you've set up Exchange, it's easy to get started:

1 Double-click on the Inbox icon on your desktop. Messages you've received (if any) will appear in your in box, as shown in Figure 13.3.

2 To read a message, double-click on it.

3 After you read a message, you can click on the appropriate button on the Exchange toolbar (or choose an option from the F_ile or E_dit menu) to print, delete, reply, or forward the message; read the next or previous message; and so forth.

FIGURE 13.3

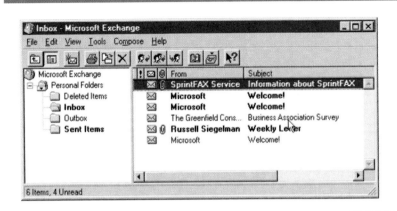

When the Inbox is selected in Microsoft Exchange, the list on the right shows newly received messages.

Getting the Most from Microsoft Exchange

Here are some tips to help you get the most from Microsoft Exchange and to help you troubleshoot problems with sending or receiving messages and faxes:

- Use the File menu to manage objects in your in box and to exit Microsoft Exchange.

- Use the View menu to show or hide the folder list, tool-bar, and status bar.

- Use the Tools menu to connect to an information ser-vice and deliver messages, maintain your address book, customize Microsoft Exchange, change properties for various information services, and so on.

- Use the Compose menu to send a new message or fax, reply to messages, and forward messages.

Anytime you're not sure what to do, pull down the Help menu in any Microsoft Exchange dialog box and explore the topics it offers. Most of your questions about using Microsoft Exchange, The Micro-soft Network, e-mail, and faxes can be answered here.

See Chapters 5 and 12 for more about printing.

- If you've set up Microsoft Fax, you can print any document to your fax modem instead of to the printer. Choose <u>F</u>ile ➤ <u>P</u>rint from your word-processing program (such as WordPad). In the Print dialog box, select Microsoft Fax as the printer and click on OK. The Compose New Fax Wizard will take over and prompt you for all the information it needs to send your document as a fax.

- Some programs (such as WordPad) offer a <u>F</u>ile ➤ Send command that lets you send the current document via network e-mail.

- To quickly fax or e-mail a document, use standard browsing techniques to find the document, right-click on that document's icon, choose Se<u>n</u>d To, and then choose Fax Recipient or Mail Recipient.

If you need help, click on the ? button at the upper-right corner of the dialog box and then click on the property you're curious about.

- If a particular information service won't work, check its properties. To do this quickly, right-click on the Inbox icon on your desktop and choose P<u>r</u>operties, click on the information service that's giving you trouble, and click on the P<u>r</u>operties button. Verify that *all* properties are set correctly on all the tabs in the Properties dialog box.

- If your faxes are rejected as *undeliverable*, try either of the following tricks:

  ◆ Right-click on the Inbox icon, choose P<u>r</u>operties, and click on the Delivery tab. Next, click on Microsoft Fax Transport in the list near the bottom of the dialog box and then click on the ↑ button until Microsoft Fax Transport moves to the top of the list. Click OK as needed.

  ◆ Create a separate profile that only includes Microsoft Fax. Then, when you're ready to send faxes, choose that profile as the default profile.

● If you have trouble with your local-area network or modem, click on the Start button, choose <u>H</u>elp, click on the Contents tab, and then open the Troubleshooting book. Choose the topic relevant to your problem.

Your best bet for getting started with Microsoft Exchange is to focus on one messaging system at a time. For example, figure out how to send and receive local e-mail, then learn how to send and receive faxes. Once you've practiced a little and taken advantage of the Windows 95 Start ➤ <u>H</u>elp and the Exchange <u>H</u>elp menus, you should be able to get everything working smoothly and efficiently.

CHAPTER 14

On the Road with Briefcase

Featuring

- Creating a new briefcase
- Loading up your briefcase
- On the road: changing your files
- Getting your files in sync
- Cleaning out your briefcase
- Other services for portable computers

On the Road Again... What do you need to pack? Along with the usual toothbrush, clothes, and papers, you'll need important files from your office computer so you can work with them while you're away. Normal luggage will be fine for those nonelectronic necessities. But for those important computer files, you can use Windows Briefcase, the electronic equivalent of a handheld briefcase.

Road warriors and anyone who lugs work home from the office will love Briefcase. The basic procedure for using Briefcase is simple:

- Create a new briefcase if you don't have one already.

- Load the briefcase with your important files and take it with you.

- While you're on the road or at home, work as you normally would but make your changes to the files in the briefcase.

- On your return, "unpack" the briefcase to update the files in your office computer and get the computers in sync.

A briefcase named *My Briefcase* appears on your desktop automatically when you install Briefcase (see *Installing Briefcase*, below). You can move *My Briefcase* to a floppy disk or to another computer's disk simply by dragging its icon from the desktop to the desired location.

Creating a New Briefcase

The first step, if you've never created a briefcase before, is to create a briefcase. (To avoid confusion, use just one briefcase). Your electronic briefcase will be like your "real" briefcase in that you'll often put things in and take things out. Therefore, you'll want to create the briefcase on your portable computer. To create a new briefcase:

1 If you'll be putting the briefcase on a floppy disk, insert the disk into your main machine's floppy drive. If your briefcase will be on a laptop or notebook computer, dock the small computer to your main machine. You need a *docking station*, a *cable*, or a *network card* to connect a laptop computer to a desktop PC.

2 Double-click on *My Computer*. Then double-click on the disk drive (and, optionally, the folder) that will contain your new briefcase.

3 Choose File ➤ New ➤ Briefcase. If the Briefcase option isn't available when you choose File ➤ New, you'll need to install Briefcase (see *Installing Briefcase*, below).

A briefcase icon will appear with the name *New Briefcase*. You can rename this icon if you wish.

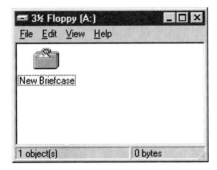

Installing Briefcase

If Briefcase isn't installed on your computer, gather the original installation disks or CD for Windows 95. Then choose Start ➤ Settings ➤ Control Panel and double-click on Add/Remove Programs. Click on the Windows Setup tab, click on Accessories, then click on the Details button. Then put a check mark next to Briefcase in the Components list. Click on OK and follow the instructions on your screen. When you're finished, put the installation disks (including any disk still in the drive) in a safe place.

Loading Up Your Briefcase

To load up your briefcase with files for the road, follow these steps:

1 If your briefcase is on a floppy disk, insert the disk into your main computer's floppy drive. If your briefcase is

All items in the briefcase must fit on a single floppy disk or on the hard disk of your laptop computer. You can't use a CD-ROM for storing briefcase files. (ROM stands for Read-Only Memory; your computer can only read from, not write to, ROM.)

Do not rename either the files or folders in the briefcase or the associated files or folders on your main machine. If you do, the renamed files will become orphaned, and updating with Briefcase will be impossible. For best results, close the briefcase windows when you're done using them. Also, make sure the floppy-disk–activity light is off before removing the floppy disk.

To find out the detailed update status for any item in the briefcase, double-click on the briefcase icon and then right-click on the file or folder you're interested in. Choose Properties, then click on the Update Status tab. Choose OK when you're finished.

To refresh the status for all files in the opened briefcase, choose View ➤ Refresh.

on a laptop or notebook, connect or dock the small computer to your main computer.

2 Double-click on the disk drive (and, if necessary, the folder) that contains your briefcase. The first time you open or use a new briefcase, a welcome message will explain the basic steps for using Briefcase. Choose Finish after reading the message.

3 Select the files or folder that should go into the briefcase and drag them onto the briefcase icon.

4 Repeat step 3 until you've put all the necessary files and folders into the briefcase. When you're done, close the briefcase windows.

Now, take your briefcase with you! Pop out the floppy disk or disconnect your laptop from your main computer, then hurry out the door.

Looking Inside the Briefcase

Anytime you want to peek inside a briefcase, double-click on its icon. If the briefcase contains folders, double-click on a folder to see what's inside. To view details about each file, choose View ➤ Details from the menu bar. The columns in the window will show the name of each file; where the original (sync) copies are located; the status of each file (Up-to-date or Needs Updating); and the size, type, and modification date for each. When you're finished looking at the briefcase, close its windows.

🖿 New Briefcase					_ □ ×
File Edit View Briefcase Help					
Name	Sync Copy In	Status	Size	Type	Modified
Bikememo	C:\Office\Wpwin	Up-to-date	6.00KB	WordPad Document	6/12/95 4:30 PM
Letter to Mom 1	C:\Windows\Desktop	Needs updating	5.00KB	WordPad Document	6/12/95 1:11 PM
Letter to Mom 2	C:\Windows\Desktop	Needs updating	4.50KB	WordPad Document	6/12/95 4:19 PM
3 object(s)					

On the Road: Changing Your Files

Once your files are safely packed into a briefcase and you're on the road (or at home), you can update the files normally. For example, double-click on the briefcase icon and any necessary folders, then double-click on a file to start its associated program; or start a program and then open a file that's in the briefcase.

If your briefcase is on a floppy disk, you can change the files directly from the floppy (though this can be slow). For faster changes, follow these steps:

1 Drag the briefcase icon from the floppy-disk window to your Windows desktop (or to a folder on your hard disk).

2 Open the briefcase, update any files as needed, save your changes, and close the files normally.

3 When you're done making changes, drag the briefcase icon back to the floppy-disk window.

4 Close all the open windows.

It's OK to use your main computer to change the original files, even if those files are stored in a briefcase. But do not change the same main *and* briefcase files, as this can confuse both you and Briefcase. If you do change both versions of a file accidentally, Briefcase will not update either version automatically (see *Getting Your Files in Sync* for more about automatic updating).

Getting Your Files in Sync

When you return to your office, you'll want to get your briefcase files in sync with those on your hard disk. Here's how:

1 If your briefcase is on a floppy disk, insert the disk into your main computer's floppy drive. If your briefcase is on a laptop or notebook computer, dock the small computer to your main machine.

2 Locate the briefcase and double-click on its icon.

3 Choose which files to update:

- To update all possible files, from the menu bar choose Briefcase ➤ Update All.

- To update selected files, select those files in the briefcase window. Then choose Briefcase ➤ Update Selection.

Update All is generally the safest choice.

4 Briefcase will figure out which files need updating.

- If all files are up-to-date, Briefcase will tell you so. Choose OK to clear the message and return to the desktop.

- If any files need to be updated, an Update dialog box will appear, as in Figure 14.1.

FIGURE 14.1

An Update dialog box tells you which files need to be updated and which files will be replaced.

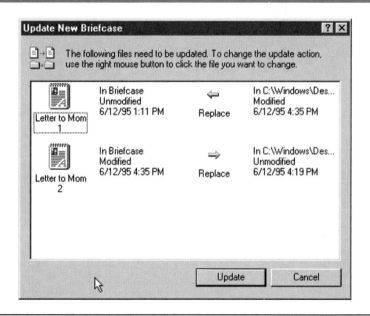

5 If you want to change how files will be updated, right-click on the file you want to change, then choose one of these options:

> → Replace The file inside the briefcase replaces the one *outside* the briefcase.
>
> ← Replace The file *outside* the briefcase replaces the one *inside* the briefcase.
>
> ↓ Skip Do not update this file at all.
>
> What's This? Explain this dialog box in more detail.

6 Repeat step 5 as needed.

7 When you're ready to update the files, click on Update.

After a short delay, the updates will be complete, and the briefcase window will show the current status of each file (all files usually will be marked as *Up-to-date*). Close the briefcase windows when you're done.

> Briefcase will select ↓ Skip automatically if both the original and briefcase copies of a file have changed.

Cleaning Out Your Briefcase

When you're finished using a briefcase, you can throw it away (by dragging it to the Recycle Bin) or keep the briefcase and reuse it later. Here are some suggestions for deciding which method might be best for you:

> It's generally easiest to delete the old briefcase and start fresh with a new one before your next trip.

● If you don't plan to update many (or any) of the files in the briefcase on your next road trip or home session, delete the old briefcase. Before your next outing, simply create a new briefcase and load it as explained in this chapter.

Don't forget to open the briefcase and choose Briefcase ➤ Update All to get all the files in sync before you and your briefcase blast out the door.

● If you plan to update most or all of the same files (and perhaps some new ones) on your next outing, reuse the old briefcase.

If you will be reusing your briefcase, remember these points:

● To add files (or folders) to the briefcase, drag them from their original location to the briefcase icon or window.

● To delete files (or folders) from the briefcase, drag them to the Recycle Bin or select them and press Delete. Choose Yes when asked for confirmation. Deleting files from a briefcase *does not* delete the original files.

● To break the connection between a file in the briefcase and the original file, click on the file in the briefcase and choose Briefcase ➤ Split From Original ➤ Yes. In the future, both files will be treated independently and will be ignored when you choose the Briefcase ➤ Update… options.

Other Services for Portable Computers

Beyond Briefcase, Windows 95 offers several other features that will interest owners of laptop computers. For more information on the services (listed below), search the Windows 95 Help index for **laptop** or for the appropriate boldface phrase in the list that follows:

Deferred Printing: Print from your laptop even when you're not hooked to a printer. When you re-dock, printing will start automatically.

Dial-Up Networking: Get complete access to your office computer or network from your laptop using a modem and standard telephone lines.

Direct Cable Connection: Hook your laptop to another computer or even an entire network with just a serial or high-speed parallel cable. No network card required!

Docking Detection: Windows 95 can automatically detect when your laptop is docked and undocked.

Power: Lets you monitor and conserve battery power.

See Chapter 12 for more details about using a network.

You road warriors and work-at-home-aholics will rest easier now that you can keep computers in sync with Briefcase and you have more access to your main computer or network via direct cable connection, deferred printing, simplified docking, and remote access.

Installing Windows 95

Featuring:

- Hardware requirements
- Installing Windows 95
- Adding optional components

If Windows 95 is already installed on your computer, you can skip this Appendix and start enjoying Windows 95 right away. If Windows 95 isn't installed, now's the time to do it. It's easy!

Your best bet is always to check the documentation that came with your Windows 95 package if you need instructions more detailed than we can offer in this appendix. You should also consult the setup.txt file on your Setup Disk 1 (or CD-ROM Setup disk) for last-minute information.

Hardware Requirements

Windows 95 requires the following hardware on your computer:

CPU: 386, 486, or Pentium processor

Memory: 4 MB minimum (but you're better off with at least 8 MB)

Disk Drives: One floppy disk or one CD-ROM drive

Free Hard-Disk Space: At least 13 megabytes for a <u>T</u>ypical setup; at least 27 megabytes to set up all components

Getting Ready to Install Windows 95

You should run Setup from MS-DOS *only* if there isn't a working version of Windows on your PC.

Microsoft strongly recommends that you run Setup from the Windows 3.1 Program Manager and that you *upgrade* your existing Windows rather than installing to a new directory.

Running Setup from Windows 3.1 offers many advantages:

- More of your hardware and software will be detected automatically.

- Setup runs faster.

- Setup requires less free memory (which makes a big difference on 4-MB machines).

Upgrading your existing version of Windows 3.1 also has many advantages:

- All your programs should work as they did before you installed Windows 95.

- You won't need to reinstall hardware devices that require Windows.

- You'll have a chance to save your Windows 3.1 and DOS system files so you can uninstall Windows 95 if you have any problems.

Before running Setup, do the following housekeeping tasks:

1 Check for and clean out any viruses on your system (you can use the MSAV program that comes with later versions of DOS).

2 Run a full surface scan on your hard disk (you can use the SCANDISK command in DOS if you don't have another hard-disk–maintenance program).

3 Make sure you aren't loading any anti-virus software (such as MSAV or another anti-virus program) by looking in autoexec.bat for lines that start anti-virus programs and in \Windows\win.ini for *run=* or *load=* lines that run an anti-virus program. If they exist, comment those lines out (or delete them). Also, remove anti-virus program icons from the Startup group in Program Manager.

4 Restart your machine, then Windows, to get a nice clean system.

5 Close all programs except Program Manager.

Installing Windows 95

Once you've finished the preliminaries, follow these steps to install Windows 95:

1 Gather your Windows 95 setup disks. These will consist of a large stack of floppy disks or one CD. (If you have floppies *and* a CD-ROM available, use your CD-ROM. It's much faster!)

Reinstall Windows 95 from scratch *only* in the unlikely event that things become hopelessly goofed up and normal trouble-shooting doesn't help.

2 Do one of the following:

- If you're upgrading from Windows 3.1, make sure you've closed all running programs except Program Manager (it's best to install Windows 95 from Program Manager).

- If you're starting from the DOS prompt because you don't have a working copy of Windows, go to the C:\> prompt.

- If you're *reinstalling* Windows 95 from scratch, choose Start ➤ Sh<u>u</u>t Down ➤ <u>R</u>estart the computer? ➤ <u>Y</u>es. When the *Starting Windows 95* message appears, press F8, choose option 6, and press ↵.

3 Insert Setup Disk 1 into the floppy or load the CD-ROM onto the CD-ROM drive.

4 If you're starting from Program Manager, choose File ➤ Run from the Program Manager menu. Then, whether you're starting from the DOS prompt or from Program Manager, type *x*:**setup** (where *x* is the drive letter that contains your setup disk). For example, type **a:setup** or **b:setup** if the setup disk is in drive A or B, respectively.

5 Press ↵.

6 Respond to any prompts that appear. When asked to choose the type of setup you want, pick one of the following:

Typical Recommended for most users. This option gives you a chance to install The Microsoft Network, Microsoft Mail, and Microsoft Fax. It also gives you a chance to choose a list of optional components to install, just as the Custom install (described below) does. If you choose not to install optional components during the Typical install, you still can install them later, as explained in Chapter 10 of this book.

Portable A slimmed-down Windows designed for portable computers.

Compact A slimmed-down Windows designed for computers that are very short on available disk space.

Custom Lets you customize all available Setup options. Recommended if you're a network administrator or advanced user, or if you want to install components of Windows that aren't usually included in a Typical setup.

7 Follow the instructions and answer any prompts that appear.

Setup will analyze your computer and take its best guess about what's there, so you shouldn't have to do much more than insert disks when Setup asks for them. If you're not sure about the answer to a prompt, choose the suggested option. You can always change things later (see Chapter 10).

After copying all the Windows 95 files, Setup will restart your computer, update a bunch of files, prompt for your network user name and password if necessary (see Chapters 2 and 12), and ask you to choose a time zone. To choose the time zone, click on your part of the world in the picture, click on Apply, and then click on OK until Windows 95 restarts your computer. Respond to additional prompts if they appear. In a few moments, a Welcome screen will appear on the Windows desktop and Windows 95 will be ready to go. Here are your options:

● Click on Close or press Escape to clear the Welcome screen.

● Click on Windows Tour to take a quick tutorial.

● Click on What's New to find out what's new in Windows 95.

● Click on Online Registration to register your Windows 95 program via your modem (if you don't have a modem, use the card that came with Windows 95 to register).

If your computer includes network hardware, you'll be prompted for a computer name, workgroup name, and computer description. These topics are covered in Chapter 12.

If you're upgrading from Windows 3.1 to Windows 95, you may wonder where your group windows and programs went. They're not lost! To find them, click on Start in the Windows 95 taskbar, then click on Programs. For more about what's new in Windows 95, see *What's New in Windows 95?* in the front of the book or click on the What's New button in the Welcome screen.

If you did a Typical, Portable, or Compact setup, or you installed from floppies, some Windows components mentioned in this book won't be set up automatically. Never fear! It's easy to add them later without re-installing Windows from scratch. You can install most optional components by following the steps under *Installing New Programs* in Chapter 10.

See Chapter 10 and the readme.txt file on Supplemental Disk 1 for more details.

Adding Optional Components Later

If you installed from floppy disks, some optional components will be on Supplemental Disk 1 rather than on the main Setup disks. These include Quick View, Character Map, Net Watcher, System Monitor, Mouse Pointers, CD Player, and Windows 95 Tour. To install components from Supplemental Disk 1:

1 Insert Windows 95 Supplemental Disk 1 into drive A or B.

2 Click on the Start button, choose Settings ➤ Control Panel, and then double-click on Add/Remove Programs.

3 Click on the Windows Setup tab.

4 Click on the Have Disk button, specify the drive that contains your floppy disk (A or B), and click on OK.

5 Click on the optional components you want to install, and then click on Install. That's all there is to it!

Index

Note to the Reader: Throughout this index **boldface** page numbers indicate primary discussions of a topic. *Italicized* page numbers indicate illustrations.

FOR EVERY COMPUTER QUESTION,
THERE IS A SYBEX BOOK THAT HAS THE ANSWER

Each computer user learns in a different way. Some need thorough, methodical explanations, while others are too busy for details. At Sybex we bring nearly 20 years of experience to developing the book that's right for you. Whatever your needs, we can help you get the most from your software and hardware, at a pace that's comfortable for you.

We start beginners out right. You will learn by seeing and doing with our **Quick & Easy** series: friendly, colorful guidebooks with screen-by-screen illustrations. For hardware novices, the **Your First** series offers valuable purchasing advice and installation support.

Often recognized for excellence in national book reviews, our **Mastering** titles are designed for the intermediate to advanced user, without leaving the beginner behind. A **Mastering** book provides the most detailed reference available. Add our pocket-sized **Instant Reference** titles for a complete guidance system. Programmers will find that the new **Developer's Handbook** series provides a more advanced perspective on developing innovative and original code.

With the breathtaking advances common in computing today comes an ever increasing demand to remain technologically up-to-date. In many of our books, we provide the added value of software, on disks or CDs. Sybex remains your source for information on software development, operating systems, networking, and every kind of desktop application. We even have books for kids. Sybex can help smooth your travels on the **Internet** and provide **Strategies and Secrets** to your favorite computer games.

As you read this book, take note of its quality. Sybex publishes books written by experts—authors chosen for their extensive topical knowledge. In fact, many are professionals working in the computer software field. In addition, each manuscript is thoroughly reviewed by our technical, editorial, and production personnel for accuracy and ease-of-use before you ever see it—our guarantee that you'll buy a quality Sybex book every time.

To manage your hardware headaches and optimize your software potential, ask for a Sybex book.

FOR MORE INFORMATION, PLEASE CONTACT:

SYBEX

Sybex Inc.
2021 Challenger Drive
Alameda, CA 94501
Tel: (510) 523-8233 • (800) 227-2346
Fax: (510) 523-2373

Sybex is committed to using natural resources wisely to preserve and improve our environment. As a leader in the computer books publishing industry, we are aware that over 40% of America's solid waste is paper. This is why we have been printing our books on recycled paper since 1982.

This year our use of recycled paper will result in the saving of more than 153,000 trees. We will lower air pollution effluents by 54,000 pounds, save 6,300,000 gallons of water, and reduce landfill by 27,000 cubic yards.

In choosing a Sybex book you are not only making a choice for the best in skills and information, you are also choosing to enhance the quality of life for all of us.